6.95

FAITH AND DOUBT IN VICTORIAN BRITAIN

CONTEXT AND COMMENTARY

Series Editor: ARTHUR POLLARD

Published Titles

Forthcoming Titles

FAITH AND DOUBT
IN VICTORIAN
BRITAIN

Elisabeth Jay

MACMILLAN

First published 1986

Published by
MACMILLAN EDUCATION LTD
Houndmills, Basingstoke, Hampshire RG21 2XS
and London
Companies and representatives
throughout the world

Typeset by Wessex Typesetters
(Division of The Eastern Press Ltd)
Frome, Somerset

Printed in Hong Kong

British Library Cataloguing in Publication Data
Jay, Elisabeth
Faith and doubt in Victorian Britain.—
(Context and commentary)
1. Great Britain—Church history—19th century
I. Title   II. Series
274.1'081   BR759

ISBN 0–333–37658–7
ISBN 0–333–37659–5 Pbk

Contents

List of Plates

1. George Eliot in 1865. A drawing in chalks by Sir Frederick Burton.
Photograph © National Portrait Gallery.

2. Frontispiece to J. Purchas *The Directorium Anglicanum* (1858). See pages 43–44.
Photograph © Bodleian Library, Oxford.

3. *Christ in the House of his Parents.* Painting by John Everett Millais, 1849–50. The composition observes the Oxford Movements' sacramental view of church architecture.
Photograph © Tate Gallery Publications.

4. *Family Prayers.* Painting by Samuel Butler, 1864. Photograph reproduced by kind permission of the Master and Fellows of St John's College, Cambridge.

5. The Metropolitan Tabernacle. See page 89.
Photograph © Bodleian Library, Oxford.

Note on the Texts

In choosing texts for this volume of Context and Commentary I have endeavoured to represent something of the variety of thought and practice within any one religious sector. This involved a mixture of seminal, and therefore better-known, texts with the less easily accessible. In selecting passages which illustrate how nineteenth-century writers imaginatively apprehended their own and others' religious faith, I have concentrated upon literary merit rather than making use of the profusion of polemically inspired poetry and fiction available.

Organising such protean concepts as 'faith' and 'doubt' into neatly divided sections carries one obvious danger: the tendency to obscure the essential fluidity of connection. Many of the writers at various periods in their lives espoused different religious positions. One work of Tennyson's, admittedly composed over seventeen years, finds a place both under Broad Church allegiances and within the realm of Doubt. John Henry Newman can be as interesting in articulating his critical reaction to a position he formerly endorsed as in his more positive statements of belief. Both John and his brother Francis were to write substantial accounts of their spiritual and intellectual journeys. The resulting books, *Phases of Faith* (1850) and *Apologia pro vita sua* (1864), make one sharply aware first of minds on the move and secondly of the agonising which accompanied the commitment to following the truth wherever it might lead. The comparative ease with which, especially in the first half of the nineteenth century, men and women effected the intellectual and social transition between the Established Church and Dissent should not lead one to assume a similar ease in transferring emotional commitments. The pursuit of doctrinal purity was a painful business, often involving material sacrifice, and the passionate or even militant nature of the 'committed' and the anguish expressed in families where conscience had decreed divergent patterns of religious allegiance are both testimony to this.

Where cross reference to another chapter might prove helpful this is indicated, at the appropriate point, by reference to the page or pages on which the relevant text appears. To clarify the chronology of the sources, references within the main text have where possible, and particularly in the case of imaginative literature, been simplified to date of composition or original publication and chapter or verse. Fuller details of the precise text used will be found in the Bibliography under Primary Sources.

Editor's Preface

J.H. Plumb has said that 'the aim of (the historian) is to understand men both as individuals and in their social relationships in time. "Social" embraces all of man's activities – economic, religious, political, artistic, legal, military, scientific – everything, indeed, that affects the life of mankind.' Literature is itself similarly comprehensive. From Terence onwards writers have embraced his dictum that all things human are their concern.

It is the aim of this series to trace the interweavings of history and literature, to show by judicious quotation and commentary how those actually working within the various fields of human activity influenced and were influenced by those who were writing the novels, poems and plays within the several periods. An attempt has been made to show the special contribution that such writers make to the understanding of their times by virtue of their peculiar imaginative 'feel' for their subjects and the intensely personal angle from which they observe the historical phenomena that provide their inspiration and come within their creative vision. In its turn the historical evidence, besides and beyond its intrinsic importance, serves to 'place' the imaginative testimony of the writers.

The authors of the several volumes in this series have sought to intermingle history and literature in the conviction that the study of each is enhanced thereby. They have been free to adopt their own approach within the broad general pattern of the series. The topics themselves have sometimes also a particular slant and emphasis. Commentary, for instance, has had to be more detailed in some cases than in others. All the contributors to the series are at one, however, in the belief (at a time when some critics would not only divorce texts from their periods but even from their authors) that literature is the creation of actual men and women, actually living in an identifiable set of historical circumstances, themselves both the creatures and the creators of their times.

ARTHUR POLLARD

For Anna and Hugo

1 The Evangelicals

Evangelicalism had its origin in the mid-eighteenth century with the spontaneous conversions of a number of isolated Anglicans living in the remoter districts of England such as Yorkshire and Cornwall. By the mid-nineteenth century the influence of its doctrine and practice had become a dominant force in Victorian religious life. Growing popularity and power sometimes resulted in a dilution of the spiritual fervour which characterised its conception until its name was in danger of becoming a synonym for bellicose political Protestantism or cultural philistinism. At heart, however, and it was to the heart's consciousness of sin and the need for Christ's redemptive power that Evangelicalism addressed itself, the essentials of Evangelical doctrine remained unchanged. An insistence on the primacy of the individual's relationship with his Saviour, maintained through prayer and the search for guidance from Scripture, allowed for considerable variation in the interpretation of these 'vital simplicities'. Moderate Calvinists and Arminians, differing upon the question of man's predestination to salvation or damnation and his consequent moral responsibility for choosing the Christian life, could both proudly proclaim themselves Evangelicals.

Inasmuch as they shared the conviction that preaching the Gospel to all was a paramount duty, Anglican Evangelicals were brought close to their Dissenting brethren but remained divided from them on the matter of the usefulness of the form and order provided by the Established Church. The tension of defending the Church Visible to those Dissenters bent upon disestablishment, whilst arguing for the supremacy of the Church Invisible of all believers against the Tractarians, at times deflected their energies into the bitterness of party warfare and away from the real strength of their practical witness of God's love through an earnest involvement with the welfare, spiritual, moral and material, of their fellow souls. The arrangement of material in this chapter has endeavoured to

1

take into account the changing fortunes and perceptions of the party without losing sight of the bedrock of its faith and practice.

We might reasonably anticipate that Evangelical insistence on the individual's significance might foster a sense of the unique response to life which sometimes finds expression in a powerful literary vision. Yet Evangelicalism has traditionally been stigmatised as a 'one book religion'. Although critics made much of Evangelicalism's reliance upon private judgement, Evangelicals would have replied that this was always to be used under the Holy Spirit's guidance to further the personal relationship with God. Just as every human faculty has been impaired by the Fall, so it was redeemed by the atoning sacrifice of Christ and might be used safely only in His service. Evangelicals have often been misrepresented as wholly opposed to the imagination and the intellect but their sermons alone would swiftly demonstrate how the imagination at least might be exercised, once sanctified in God's service, to warn the sinner or comfort the penitent.

Religious poetry received Protestant sanction in Milton's genius and Evangelical authority in the poems and hymns of Cowper, a poet recognised far beyond Evangelical circles. Hymns, which proved so useful a mnemonic device for instilling doctrine, could be seen to have direct devotional application.

Evangelical Faith: 'Believe and be saved'

This earnest appeal to conversion appears in *A Practical View of the Prevailing Religious System of Professed Christians, in the Higher and Middle Classes in this country, contrasted with real Christianity* (1797) which continued to be popular Evangelical reading well into the nineteenth century.

> If there be any one who is inclined to listen to this solemn warning, who is awakened from his dream of false security, and is disposed to be not only *almost* but *altogether* a christian – O! let him not stifle or dissipate these beginnings of seriousness, but sedulously cherish

them as the "workings of the Divine Spirit," which would draw him from the "broad" and crowded "road of destruction into the narrow" and thinly peopled path "that leadeth to life." Let him retire from the multitude – let him enter into his closet, and on his bended knees implore, for Christ's sake and in reliance on his mediation, that God would "take away from him the heart of stone, and give him a heart of flesh;" that the Father of light would open his eyes to his true condition, and clear his heart from the clouds of prejudice, and dissipate the deceitful medium of self-love. Then let him carefully examine his past life, and his present course of conduct, comparing himself with God's word: and considering how any one might reasonably have been expected to conduct himself, to whom the holy scriptures had been always open, and who had been used to acknowledge them to be the revelation of the will of his Creator, and Governor, and Supreme Benefactor; let him there peruse the awful denunciations against impenitent sinners; let him labour to become more and more deeply impressed with a sense of his own radical blindness and corruption; above all, let him steadily contemplate, in all its bearings and connexions, that stupendous truth, *the incarnation and crucifixion of the only begotten Son of God, and the message of mercy proclaimed from the cross to repenting sinners.* – "Be ye reconciled unto God." – "Believe in the Lord Jesus Christ, and thou shalt be saved."

When he fairly estimates the guilt of sin by the costly satisfaction which was required to atone for it, and the worth of his soul by the price which was paid for its redemption, and contrasts both of these with his own sottish inconsiderateness; when he reflects on the amazing love and pity of Christ, and on the cold and formal acknowledgments with which he has hitherto returned this infinite obligation, making light of the precious blood of the Son of God, and trifling with the gracious invitations of his Redeemer; surely, if he be not lost to sensibility, mixed emotions of guilt, and fear, and shame, and remorse, and sorrow, will nearly overwhelm his soul; he will smite upon his breast, and cry out in the language of the publican, "God be merciful to me a sinner." But, blessed be God, such an one needs not despair: it is to persons in this very situation, and with these very feelings, that the offers of the gospel are held forth, and its promises assured; "to the weary and heavy laden" under the burden of their sins; to those who thirst for the water of life; to those who feel themselves "tied and bound by the chain of their sins;" who abhor their captivity, and long earnestly for deliverance. Happy, happy souls! which the grace of God has visited, "has brought out of darkness into his marvellous light," and "from the power of Satan unto God." Cast yourselves then on his undeserved mercy; he is full of love, and will not spurn you: surrender yourselves into his hands, and solemnly resolve, through his grace, to dedicate henceforth all your faculties and powers to his service.

It is yours now "to work out your own salvation with fear and trembling," relying on the fidelity of Him who has promised to "work in you both to will and to do of his good pleasure." Ever look to him for help: your only safety consists in a deep and abiding sense of your own weakness, and in a firm reliance on his strength.

W. Wilberforce, *A Practical View* (1797),
pp.441-44.

Whilst personal conviction of the supreme importance of total surrender and commitment to Christ produces an emotional rhetoric, this is balanced by language advocating quiet meditation in which reason will play its part in revealing man's sin. Himself a member of Britain's governing elite, Wilberforce deploys a sense of social impropriety ('sottish inconsiderateness') to awaken the reader's shame before offering the comforts of the Bible's plan of salvation. Conversion is pictured here as a gradual process, resulting in a life of active service, not as an isolated moment of violent emotion.

For some it proved impossible to hold 'a sense of your own weakness and . . . a firm reliance on his strength' in spiritually profitable tension. The life and poetry of William Cowper (1731–1800) oscillated between the state of comfortable 'divine chit-chat' found in 'The Task' and the recurrent conviction, expressed in poems like 'The Castaway', that he had been everlastingly damned by God. Those like the Brontë children, on the other hand, who had been brought up to believe in a salvation freely available to all, reacted strongly to their encounter with the Calvinist strain of Evangelicalism. Charlotte, who probably first encountered such teaching at school, briefly succumbed to such despair and Anne displays vivid insight into its psychological horrors in a poem reassessing the implications of Cowper's poetry which, as a child, she had merely used as a channel for her own feelings. Even her central conviction in a God of love cannot entirely dismiss the possibility of eternal damnation.

> Sweet are thy strains, Celestial Bard,
>   And oft in childhood's years
> I've read them o'er and o'er again
>   With floods of silent tears.
>
> The language of my inmost heart
>   I traced in every line –
> *My* sins, *my* sorrows, hopes and fears
>   Were there, and only mine.
>
> All for myself the sigh would swell,
>   The tear of anguish start;
> I little knew what wilder woe
>   Had filled the poet's heart.
>
> I did not know the nights of gloom,
>   The days of misery,
> The long long years of dark despair
>   That crushed and tortured thee.

But they are gone, and now from earth
Thy gentle soul is passed.
And in the bosom of its God
Has found its Home at last.

It must be so if God is love
And answers fervent prayer;
Then surely thou shalt dwell on high,
And I may meet thee there.

⁎   ⁎   ⁎

Yet should thy darkest fears be true,
If Heaven be so severe
That such a soul as thine is lost,
O! how shall I appear?

A. Brontë, 'To Cowper' (1842), vv.1-6; 11.

The Changing Historical Perspective

The divergence of doctrinal opinion possible in a religious
system which placed such emphasis upon the authority of
individual judgement became increasingly manifest as the
party grew in numerical strength and re-encountered problems
which had been shelved rather than solved in the eighteenth
century. As an Evangelical by upbringing and, by 1839, a
leading member of the Oxford Movement's endeavours to
reassert the spiritual authority of the Church's teaching (see
pp.26–27), John Henry Newman repeatedly attacked
Evangelicalism for its incapacity to counter the growth of
liberalism, either in its political aspect of reforms which
seemed poised to disestablish the Church of England itself or
in its intellectual aspect, where rationalism allowed no appeal
to the authority of tradition. Only by asserting Anglicanism's
Catholic inheritance against the Protestant strain imported by
sixteenth-century Reformers from the continental teachings of
Zwingli or Melanchthon could the *via media*, upon which
Anglicanism's existence then appeared to Newman to depend,
be assured.

Its adherents are already separating from each other, and it is not difficult to see that in due time they will melt away like a snow drift. Indeed their very success would cause this result, if there were no other reason. The possession of power naturally tends to the dissolution of all confidence; how much more so then in the case of a party, which is not only open to the wilfulnesses and rivalries of our frail nature, but which actually sanctifies them by propounding as a first principle that in spirituals no man is really above another, but that each individual, from high to low, is both privileged and bound to make out his religious views for himself? But over and above this, the system in question, if so it may be called, is, as we have intimated, full of inconsistencies and anomalies; it is built not on one principle but on half a dozen; and thus contains within it the seeds of ruin, which time only is required to develope.

It has no straight-forward view on any one point on which it professes to teach; and to hide its poverty it has dressed itself out in a maze of words, which all enquirers feel and are perplexed with, yet few are able to penetrate. It cannot pronounce plainly what it holds about the sacraments, what it means by unity, what it thinks of antiquity, what fundamentals are, what the Church; what again it means by faith. It has no intelligible rule for interpreting Scripture beyond that of submission to the arbitrary comments which have come down to it, though it knows it not, from Zuingle or Melanchthon. "Unstable as water it cannot excel." It is but an inchoate state or stage of a doctrine, and its final resolution is in rationalism. This it has ever shown when suffered to work itself out without interruption; and among ourselves it is only kept from doing so by the influence of our received formularies. When then it is confronted, as now it is more and more likely to be, by more consistent views, it cannot maintain its present unscientific condition. It will either disappear or be carried out. Some of its adherents will be startled and return to sounder views; others will develope themselves into avowed liberalism. Its many societies and institutions, however well organized and energetic, will avail it nothing in this crisis. They are but framework and machinery, and while they presuppose a creed they are available for one almost as much as the other. . . . Thus the matter stands as regards the far spread religious confederacy of our days. We have no dread of it at all; we only fear what it may lead to. It does not stand on entrenched ground or make any pretence to a position; it does but occupy the μεταίχμιον, the space between contending powers, Catholic truth and rationalism.

> J.H. Newman, 'The State of Religious Parties',
> *The British Critic* (April 1839), pp.418–19.

Looking back from the vantage point of the 1850s, George Eliot was inclined to share Newman's conviction that the mid-1830s had witnessed the Evangelical Movement's watershed. In terms of spiritual efficacy she may well have been correct but diagnoses offered by Newman, Eliot, Trollope and Butler in conjunction with one another should encourage a healthy scepticism about the apparent objectivity of such assessments. Newman had been anxious to sound Evangelicalism's death knell in order to realign the battle formation. In the 1830s George Eliot had experienced a fervent Evangelical faith which she subsequently found it impossible to sustain in the face of the new Biblical criticism (see pp.102–105). The religion of Humanity which she then embraced prompted her, nevertheless, to acknowledge the moral worth of much of the movement's work and to employ her fiction to win from her readers a sympathetic awareness of the inner lives of those often dismissed by popular prejudice.

It was soon notorious in Milby that Mr Tryan held peculiar opinions; that he preached extempore; that he was founding a religious lending library in his remote corner of the parish; that he expounded the Scriptures in cottages; and that his preaching was attracting the Dissenters, and filling the very aisles of his church. The

rumour sprang up that Evangelicalism had invaded
Milby parish – a murrain or blight all the more terrible,
because its nature was but dimly conjectured. Perhaps
Milby was one of the last spots to be reached by the
wave of a new movement; and it was only now, when
the tide was just on the turn, that the limpets there got a
sprinkling. Mr Tryan was the first Evangelical
clergyman who had risen above the Milby horizon:
hitherto that obnoxious adjective had been unknown to
the townspeople of any gentility; and there were even
many Dissenters who considered "evangelical" simply
a sort of baptismal name to the magazine which
circulated among the congregation of Salem Chapel.
But now, at length, the disease had been imported,
when the parishioners were expecting it as little as the
innocent Red Indians expected smallpox. As long as Mr
Tryan's hearers were confined to Paddiford Common –
which, by the by, was hardly recognisable as a common
at all, but was a dismal district where you heard the
rattle of the hand-loom, and breathed the smoke of
coal-pits – the "canting parson" could be treated as a
joke. Not so when a number of single ladies in the town
appeared to be infected, and even one or two men of
substantial property, with old Mr Landor, the banker,
at their head, seemed to be "giving in" to the new
movement – when Mr Tryan was known to be well
received in several good houses, where he was in the
habit of finishing the evening with exhortation and
prayer. Evangelicalism was no longer a nuisance
existing merely in by-corners, which any well-clad
person could avoid; it was invading the very drawing-
rooms, mingling itself with the comfortable fumes of
port-wine and brandy, threatening to deaden with its
murky breath all the splendour of the ostrich feathers,
and to stifle Milby ingenuousness, not pretending to be
better than its neighbours, with a cloud of cant and
lugubrious hypocrisy. The alarm reached its climax
when it was reported that Mr Tryan was endeavouring
to obtain authority from Mr Prendergast, the non-
resident rector, to establish a Sunday evening lecture in

the parish church, on the ground that old Mr Crewe did
not preach the Gospel.

G. Eliot, 'Janet's Repentance' (1857), *Scenes of
Clerical Life*, Ch. 2.

Trollope's fictional portrait of an Evangelical cleric, penned
in 1857, the same year that saw Mr Tryan's creation, employs
similar tactics to arouse anti-Evangelical prejudice as the
inhabitants of Milby had done. Mr Slope and Mr Tryan share a
preference for spontaneous forms of worship, suggestive of
Dissent, and are fearless in pleading their cause in a manner that
seems to threaten the easy ways of normal social intercourse.

> In doctrine, he [Mr. Slope], like his patron, is tolerant
> of dissent, if so strict a mind can be called tolerant of
> anything. With Wesleyan-Methodists he has something
> in common, but his soul trembles in agony at the
> iniquities of the Puseyites. His aversion is carried to
> things outward as well as inward. His gall rises at a new
> church with a high-pitched roof; a full-breasted black
> silk waistcoat is with him a symbol of Satan; and a
> profane jest-book would not, in his view, more foully
> desecrate the church seat of a Christian, than a book of
> prayer printed with red letters, and ornamented with a
> cross on the back. Most active clergymen have their
> hobby, and Sunday observances are his. Sunday,
> however, is a word which never pollutes his mouth – it
> is always "the Sabbath." The "desecration of the
> Sabbath," as he delights to call it, is to him meat and
> drink: – he thrives upon that as policemen do on the
> general evil habits of the community. It is the loved
> subject of all his evening discourses, the source of all his
> eloquence, the secret of all his power over the female
> heart. To him the revelation of God appears only in that
> one law given for Jewish observance. To him the
> mercies of our Saviour speak in vain, to him in vain has
> been preached that sermon which fell from divine lips
> on the mountain – "Blessed are the meek, for they shall
> inherit the earth" – "Blessed are the merciful, for they

shall obtain mercy." To him the New Testament is comparatively of little moment, for from it can he draw no fresh authority for that dominion which he loves to exercise over at least a seventh part of man's allotted time here below.

Mr. Slope is tall, and not ill made. . . . His face is nearly of the same colour as his hair, though perhaps a little redder: it is not unlike beef – beef, however, one would say, of a bad quality. His forehead is capacious and high, but square and heavy, and unpleasantly shining. His mouth is large, though his lips are thin and bloodless; and his big, prominent, pale brown eyes inspire anything but confidence. His nose, however, is his redeeming feature: it is pronounced straight and well-formed; though I myself should have liked it better did it not possess a somewhat spongy, porous appearance, as though it had been cleverly formed out of a red coloured cork.

I never could endure to shake hands with Mr. Slope. A cold, clammy perspiration always exudes from him, the small drops are ever to be seen standing on his brow, and his friendly grasp is unpleasant.

A. Trollope, Barchester Towers (1857), Ch. 4.

Trollope, who had been brought up to dislike Evangelicals and believed them to be gaining ever-increasing ecclesiastical power, shamelessly exploits those very prejudices George Eliot had sought to counteract. Slope is an arrogant social climber with a repulsive demeanour, for neither of which features his doctrines can justly be blamed. Tryan was created in a mirror-image of such stereotypes, rejecting the wealthy life to which he was born to live and work amongst the poor in constant self-mortification. Despite its worthy intentions George Eliot's portrayal of Tryan does not really challenge the stereotype but rather provides a more attractive alternative. For a successful challenge the reader should look elsewhere in her work, notably to 'The Sad Fortunes of the Reverend Amos Barton', a picture of an ill-educated, self-important, ugly clergyman, or to the lengthy and intricate exploration of the emotional and social needs which draw Bulstrode to Evangelicalism in *Middlemarch*.

A further picture of the poverty-stricken fraternity from which the likes of Slope emerge with the aid of a subsidised university education can be found in Samuel Butler's *The Way of All Flesh* (1903), Ch. 47 (see also pp.125–26) which describes the Cambridge haunts of the 'Simeonites', so nicknamed after their influential patron, the Rev. Charles Simeon (1759–1836), incumbent of Holy Trinity, Cambridge. Butler's posthumously published novel talks mainly of Evangelicalism in the 1830s, 40s and 50s, locating the Cambridge episode in 1858; but whereas Trollope had identified this as a period of Evangelicalism triumphant, Butler, like Eliot, was led by personal bias to depict the religion of his childhood as a spent force.

Such evidence as one can glean from the records of various religious societies and from clerical appointments of the day suggest that, despite Newman's predictions, 'the religious confederacy' of Evangelicalism combined with popular, anti-Catholic Protestantism had not melted away 'like a snow drift' but had established itself as a powerful force within the world of Anglican politics by the second half of the nineteenth century.

As 'Prince of the Tract Writers', whose circulation figures numbered some twelve million, J.C. Ryle's militant proselytising had contributed to the general spread of Evangelical influence and his elevation to the see of Liverpool in 1880 offered further confirmation of Evangelicalism's transformation, politically speaking, from the persecuted minority of early days, relying heavily upon the patronage of prominent men like Wilberforce, to a broadly-based, powerful force demanding appropriate recognition. Ryle's definition of Evangelical doctrine is not so much an appeal to the individual soul as a party programme. The Bible, rather than original sin or conversion, is seen here as the bedrock of Evangelicalism because it provides the base for attack upon two distinct foes. The teaching of liberal theologians and scholars can be dismissed rather than debated by asserting the Bible's supremacy. Tractarian efforts to reawaken a sense of the Church's divinely appointed order is represented as an error endangering men's souls by directing their attention to means rather than ends.

(*a*) The first leading feature in Evangelical Religion is the *absolute supremacy it assigns to Holy Scripture*, as the only rule of faith and practice, the only test of truth, the only judge of controversy.

Its theory is that man is required to believe nothing, as necessary to salvation, which is not read in God's Word written or can be proved thereby. It totally denies that there is any other guide for man's soul, co-equal or co-ordinate with the Bible. It refuses to listen to such arguments as "the Church says so," – "the Fathers say so," – "primitive antiquity says so," – "Catholic tradition says so," – "the Councils say so."

The supreme authority of the Bible is one of the cornerstones of our system. Our faith can find no resting-place except in the Bible, or in Bible arguments. Here is rock: all else is sand.

(*b*) The second leading feature in Evangelical Religion is the prominence it assigns to the doctrine of human sinfulness and corruption.

Its theory is that in consequence of Adam's fall, all men are as far as possible gone from original righteousness, and are of their own natures inclined to evil. They are not only in a miserable, pitiable, and bankrupt condition, but in a state of guilt, imminent danger, and condemnation before God. They are not only at enmity with their Maker, but they have no will to serve their Maker, no love to their Maker, and no meetness for heaven.

We hold that a mighty spiritual disease like this requires a mighty spiritual medicine for its cure. We dread fostering man's favourite notion that a little church-going and sacrament-receiving, – a little patching, and mending, and whitewashing, – is all that his case requires. *Hence we protest with all our heart against formalism, sacramentalism, and every species of mere external or vicarious Christianity.* We maintain that all such religion is founded on an inadequate view of man's spiritual need. It requires far more than this to save, or satisfy, or sanctify a soul. *It requires nothing less than the blood of God the Son applied to the conscience, and the grace of God the Holy Ghost entirely renewing the heart.* Man is radically diseased, and man needs a radical cure. I believe that ignorance of the extent of the fall, and of the whole doctrine of original sin, is one grand reason why many can neither understand, appreciate, nor receive Evangelical Religion. Next to the Bible, as its foundation, it is based on a clear view of original sin.

(c) The third leading feature of Evangelical Religion is the paramount importance it attaches to the work and office of our Lord Jesus Christ, and to the nature of the salvation which He has wrought out for man.

Its theory is that the eternal Son of God, Jesus Christ, has by His life, death, and resurrection, as our Representative and Substitute, obtained a complete salvation for sinners, and a redemption from the guilt, power, and consequences of sin, and that all who believe on Him are, even while they live, completely forgiven and justified from all things, – are reckoned completely righteous before God, – are interested in Christ and all His benefits.

We hold that nothing whatever is needed between the soul of man the sinner and Christ the Saviour, but simple, childlike faith, and that all means, helps, ministers, and ordinances are useful just so far as they help this faith, but no further; – but that rested in and relied on as ends and not as means, they become harmful to the soul. . . .

Hence we maintain that people ought to be continually warned not to make a Christ of the Church, or of the ministry, or of the forms of worship, or of baptism, or of the Lord's Supper. We say that life eternal is to know Christ, believe in Christ, abide in Christ, have daily heart communion with Christ, by simple personal faith, – and that everything in religion is useful so far as it helps forward that life of faith, but no further.

(*d*) The fourth leading feature in Evangelical Religion is the *high place which it assigns to the inward work of the Holy Spirit in the heart of man.*

Its theory is that the root and foundation of all vital Christianity in any one, is a work of grace in the heart, and that until there is real experimental business within a man, his religion is a mere husk, and shell, and can neither comfort nor save. We maintain that the things which need most to be pressed on men's attention are those mighty works of the Holy Spirit, inward repentance, inward faith, inward hope, inward hatred of sin, and inward love to God's law. And we say that to tell men to take comfort in their baptism or Church-membership, when these all-important graces are unknown, is delusive and dangerous.

We hold that the witness of the Spirit, however much it may be abused, is a real true thing.

(*e*) The fifth and last leading feature in Evangelical Religion is *the importance which it attaches to the outward and visible work of the Holy Ghost in the life of man.*

Its theory is that the true grace of God is a thing that will always make itself *manifest* in the conduct, behaviour, ways and habits of him who has it. Where the Spirit is, He will always make His presence known.

We hold that it is wrong to tell men that they are "children of God and members of Christ, and heirs of the kingdom of heaven," unless they really overcome the world, the flesh, and the devil. We maintain that to tell a man he is "born of God," or regenerated, while he is living in carelessness or sin, is a dangerous delusion, and calculated to do infinite mischief to his soul. We affirm confidently that "fruit" is the only certain evidence of a man's spiritual condition; that if we would know whose he is and whom he serves, we must look first at his life.

J.C. Ryle, *Evangelical Religion: what it is, and what it is not* (1867), pp.10-13.

Practical Piety

Lord Shaftesbury, perceived by many from the 1840s as the leader of the Evangelical party, sometimes felt that it had become so broadly based as to have lost all doctrinal coherence. One certainty, however, he shared with Ryle – the vital importance of the 'outward and visible work of the Holy Ghost in the life of man'. A sense of personal accountability to God for one's fellow souls provided the inspirational force behind a host of nineteenth-century charitable societies. The significance given to personal judgement and endeavour challenged, on the one hand, the apparent indifference to individual need which accompanied the industrialisation of society and, on the other hand, the tendency to leave moral leadership to the Church hierarchy. It is no accident that two of the best remembered Evangelicals, Wilberforce and Shaftesbury, were members of the laity.

> I have asked what is your security for your belief, and I have stated that I believe it to be in the devout and simple reverence of the word of God, as indeed it is. And what is your security for your own conduct? I believe that it lies here – a deep, earnest, solemn sense of direct and individual responsibility in every man and woman born into this world. I know no sentiment that so tends to exalt, and at the same time so tends to humble the human heart, as does the sense of direct and immediate responsibility to Almighty God. If you consider yourselves in relation to man, and consider the duties you owe to your fellow-men, the purpose for which you were sent on earth, the duties you have to perform – to defend the fatherless, to plead for the widow, to enlighten the ignorant, to solace the suffering, to spread the knowledge of God among those who know it not, and to give a helping hand to all in need – if you have ever before you that sense of responsibility to man, will it not tend to urge you forward in the daily discharge of that duty? and if other men were to place these principles perpetually before them, would it not urge them forward also in the

discharge of their duties towards you? Now, look higher; regard yourselves in the light of responsible beings to Almighty God, and see how it lifts the whole mass; and though you may still continue to regard yourselves as units among the many millions, yet you are units to every one of whom God has given gifts of which sooner or later you will be called upon to render an account. I cannot conceive of anything that will tend more to regulate your conduct, govern your hopes, and exalt your desires, than the sense of individual responsibility. Ay, it has also this good effect – have you not often heard many persons exclaim, when urged to do some good in their generation, "Why, what can I do? I am a poor insignificant person; it is not in my power to do good to any one; I must hold on my course, because I am utterly powerless." If such a person was governed by a sense of deep responsibility to Almighty God, that person – be it man or woman – would perceive that he has been sent into this world for some purpose, and that purpose must be fulfilled – that he has been endowed with gifts to carry it into effect – and that, if that be not done, a frightful and fearful account must be required in the end. The more I think of it the more I am convinced that is the best guarantee for your conduct; and I rejoice to inculcate it on the mind of every one who listens to me, whatever his destination in life. When you come to stand before the great judgement–seat of God, the responsibility of every one – of the sweeper of the crossing, the shopman, or the excavator, will be just as certain and minute as the responsibility of Queen Victoria, who sits upon the throne of England.

Speeches of the Earl of Shaftesbury (1856),
pp.305–306.

Equality of opportunity for Christian service rather than a vision of social democracy was the platform upon which Shaftesbury based this rousing call to the tenth annual meeting of the Manchester Young Men's Christian Association.

Shaftesbury lived in ever-expectant hope of witnessing Christ's Second Coming, but this never weakened his efforts to ameliorate the present conditions of the poor.

Shaftesbury's theocentric vision of life found poetic expression in a hymn by Frances Ridley Havergal (1836–79), a prolific Evangelical poetess who also possessed considerable musical talent. The hymn makes allusive use both of the Bible (e.g. verse 4: cf. Isaiah 52:7) and of the Anglican liturgy. The prefatory quotation is taken from the prayer of rededication which follows the celebration of Holy Communion in the Anglican Prayer Book. The powerful battle waged between self and God is apparent in these cumulative stanzas where *my* and *I* are repeatedly subordinated to the force of the initial *Take*. The flexibility of rhythm which she achieves within the constraints of these short couplets raises the piece above the religious doggerel into which it might easily have fallen. Although it enjoyed a vogue as a Revivalist hymn, it has survived as a piece of Christian poetry which transcends sectarian boundaries.

'Here we offer and present unto Thee, O Lord, ourselves, our souls and bodies, to be a reasonable, holy, and lively sacrifice unto Thee.'

TAKE my life, and let it be
Consecrated, Lord, to Thee.

Take my moments and my days;
Let them flow in ceaseless praise.

Take my hands, and let them move
At the impulse of Thy love.

Take my feet, and let them be
Swift and 'beautiful' for Thee.

Take my voice, and let me sing
Always, only, for my King.

Take my lips, and let them be
Filled with messages from Thee.

Take my silver and my gold;
Not a mite would I withhold.

Take my intellect, and use
Every power as Thou shalt choose.

Take my will, and make it Thine;
It shall be no longer mine.

Take my heart, it *is* Thine own;
It shall be Thy royal throne.

Take my love; my Lord, I pour
At Thy feet its treasure-store.

Take myself, and I will be
Ever, *only*, ALL for Thee.

F.R. Havergal, 'Consecration Hymn' (1874).

Evangelicalism's strength relied upon the wholesale commitment of the kind embodied in this hymn. Practised as a formal system, it could result in the repressive sanctimoniousness, entirely at odds with the service of a God of Love. This is evident in the scene from *Jane Eyre*, where Mr Brocklehurst, sole treasurer and inspector of an Evangelical charity school for orphan girls, sees accountability not, like Shaftesbury, as emanating from self-examination but in terms of regulating the lives of others.

"Madam, allow me an instant! – You are aware that my plan in bringing up these girls is not to accustom them to habits of luxury and indulgence, but to render them hardy, patient, self-denying. Should any little accidental disappointment of the appetite occur, such as the spoiling of a meal, the under or the over-dressing of a dish, the incident ought not to be neutralized by replacing with something more delicate the comfort lost, thus pampering the body and obviating the aim of this institution; it ought to be improved to the spiritual edification of the pupils, by encouraging them to evince fortitude under the temporary privation. A brief address on those occasions would not be mistimed, wherein a judicious instructor would take the opportunity of referring to the sufferings of the primitive Christians; to the torments of martyrs; to the exhortations of our blessed Lord Himself, calling upon His disciples to take up their cross and follow Him; to His warnings that man shall not live by bread alone, but by every word that proceedeth out of the mouth of God; to His divine consolations, 'If ye suffer hunger or thirst for My sake, happy are ye.' Oh, madam, when you put bread and cheese, instead of burnt porridge, into these children's mouths, you may indeed feed their vile bodies, but you little think how you starve their immortal souls!" . . .

"Miss Temple, Miss Temple, what – *what* is that girl with curled hair? Red hair, ma'am, curled – curled all over?" And extending his cane he pointed to the awful object, his hand shaking as he did so.

"It is Julia Severn," replied Miss Temple, very quietly.

"Julia Severn, ma'am! And why has she, or any other, curled hair? Why, in defiance of every precept and principle of this house, does she conform to the world so openly – here, in an evangelical, charitable establishment – as to wear her hair one mass of curls?"

"Julia's hair curls naturally," returned Miss Temple, still more quietly.

"Naturally! Yes, but we are not to conform to nature. I wish these girls to be the children of Grace; and why that abundance? I have again and again intimated that I desire the hair to be arranged closely, modestly, plainly. Miss Temple, that girl's hair must be cut off entirely; I will send a barber to-morrow; and I see others who have far too much of the excrescence – that tall girl, tell her to turn round.

C. Brontë, *Jane Eyre* (1847), Ch. 7.

Brocklehurst's spiritual nullity is further underlined by his concentration upon external matters. Charlotte Brontë actually weakens the logical case against him as a representative of a particular version of Evangelicalism when she suggests hypocrisy by introducing his fashionably attired and elegantly coiffed wife and daughters immediately after this scene. She relies, however, not upon the reader's sense of logic but upon his sympathy for the child's instinctive recognition of a religious argot devoid of religious feeling. To the child's view of Brocklehurst as tyrannical ogre is added the adult perception of his absurdity. Brocklehurst's misapplied theological vocabulary makes him appear foolish but behind the ambiguity of that word 'naturally' lies a serious debate between a doctrine valuing nature as an aspect of God's revelation and a doctrine which sees in nature only evidence of the Fall.

Despite the satirical pictures which abound in Victorian novels of Evangelical upbringing as an experience of emotional anguish and repression, where tyranny masqueraded as the exercise of accountability, there are also affectionate recollections on record. George William Erskine Russell (1853–1919), nephew of a Whig prime minister, retained an admiration for the values of his Evangelical upbringing, although he later changed his allegiance to the High Church party.

> From our very earliest years we were taught the Bible, at first orally; and later we were encouraged to read it, by gifts of handsomely bound copies. I remember that our aids to study were Adam Clarke's Commentary, Nicholl's "Helps to Reading the Bible," and a book called "Light in the Dwelling." Hymns played a great part in our training. As soon as we could speak we learned "When rising from the bed of death" and "Beautiful Zion built above"; "Rock of Ages" and "Jesu, Lover of my soul" were soon added. The Catechism we were never taught. I was confirmed without learning it. It was said to be too difficult; of course, it really was too Sacramental. By way of an easier exercise I was constrained to learn the "Shorter

Catechism of the General Assembly of Divines at Westminster"! We had Family Prayers twice every day. My father read a chapter, very much as the fancy took him, or where the Bible opened of itself; and he read without note or comment. I remember a very distinct impression on my infant mind that the portions of the Bible which were read at Prayers had no meaning, and that the public reading of the words, without reference to sense, was an act of piety. After the chapter, my father read one of "Thornton's Family Prayers," and, indeed, the use of that book was a distinctive sign of true Evangelicalism. Some friends of ours tried extempore prayers, and one worthy baronet went so far as to invite contributions from the servants. As long as only the butler and the housekeeper voiced the aspirations of their fellows, all was decorous; but one fine day an insubordinate kitchen-maid took up her parable, saying, "And we pray for Sir Thomas and her Ladyship too. Oh, may they have new hearts given to them!" The bare idea that there was room for such renovation caused a prompt return to the lively oracles of Henry Thornton.

While we were still very young children, we were carefully incited to acts of practical charity. We began by carrying dinners to the sick and aged poor; then we went on to reading hymns and bits of Bible to the blind and unlettered. As soon as we were old enough, we became teachers in Sunday Schools, and conducted classes and cottage-meetings. From the very beginning we were taught to save up our money for good causes. Each of us had a "missionary-box"; and I remember another box, in the counterfeit presentment of a Gothic church, which received contributions for the Church Pastoral Aid Society.

G.W.E. Russell, *The Household of Faith* (1902), pp.240-42.

In retrospect the Dissenting origins of the commentaries, hymns and, above all, the Presbyterian catechism, all smacked too clearly of Evangelicalism's tendency to pay scant regard to the Church's order and teaching. Subscription to the Church Pastoral Aid Society (founded in 1836), which provided lay helpers for parochial clergy, was felt by High Churchmen to indicate blatant disregard for the apostolic authority of the priesthood. Furthermore, as part of their endeavour to replace formal devotions and church attendance with meaningful acts of devotion and instruction, Evangelicals had popularised the daily saying of family prayers beyond those sanctioned by the Anglican liturgy. Whilst the immediate family and servants still formed the most pressing sphere in which to spread the Gospel message, even this duty remained second to the exercise of private judgement, under the Holy Spirit's guidance, in Bible reading and soul-searching. Russell's description of his own family goes far in identifying those central elements of the Evangelical life which the Oxford Movement was to diagnose as offering the greatest threat to the authority of the Church.

2 The Oxford Movement and the Catholic Tradition

The turbulence and reforming zeal which the Great Reform Bill of 1832 seemed to promise was felt in the religious as well as the political world. By virtue of their known cooperation with Dissenters, Evangelicals seemed ill-equipped to defend the 'Church in danger' from the threats of a reforming parliament and, given their scant regard for doctrine and heavy reliance on individual judgement, even less prepared to do battle with the forces of Rationalism.

Drawn together by their common desire to defend the Anglican Church as the true heir of the Universal Catholic Church, a divinely appointed order, instituted by Christ and His apostles, a group of Oxford men combined forces to produce a series of tracts alerting their brother clergy to the critical state of the Church of England. Their attempt to test the formularies (Anglican doctrine as set out in the Prayer Book, Homilies and Articles) of the contemporary Church by reference to the teaching and practice of the Ancient Church focused attention on matters of doctrine in a way which was to prove unexpectedly unsettling. Whilst John Keble believed that he was merely continuing to defend the best of Anglican High Church tradition as he had received it from his father, John Henry Newman, who had already moved away from his early Evangelical persuasion, eventually found himself dissatisfied with the *via media* compromise between Protestantism and Rome and seceded to the Church of Rome in 1845.

The exhumation of doctrines long accepted or tacitly ignored led many to question the precise nature of their belief, others to question the belief itself, whilst others still were severely shaken by the blow Newman's secession appeared to strike against the authority which Tractarian reliance on the Church's teaching had seemed to offer.

Yet the impetus behind the Oxford Movement had never been merely intellectual. For the Tractarian the defence of the faith was related to a way of believing and a way of living. Only a life of devotion, attained through the Church's sanctioned modes of prayer and sacramental worship, leading to penitence and the pursuit of holiness, could enable the believer to attain glimpses of God's mysterious presence in His universe. Imaginative literature seemed to be fostered by one particular Tractarian doctrine. The doctrine of Reserve in communicating religious knowledge discouraged the explicit preaching which marred so much contemporary, religiously inspired literature in favour of showing God's presence obliquely as revealed in nature or in the Christian life in action. It seems more than the coincidence of a shared cultural inheritance that made three of the leading Tractarians poets of contemporary note. Newman, who later also turned his hand to novel writing, Keble and Isaac Williams all wrote poetry which reflects the way in which they perceived both the language of the Bible and nature as yielding images and types through which God had chosen to reveal Himself.

The Movement's eventual legacy was to be seen in the pastoral work of succeeding generations of Tractarians – influenced priests, the life of newly founded religious communities and the Gothic architecture of newly-endowed churches which sprang up in deprived urban areas. At the doctrinal level Tractarianism contributed to an understanding of the Church as a living organism, safeguarding both the continuity and the change necessary to such a vision against the arbitrary whims of fashionable ideologies or personal predilections.

The Tractarian 'Temper of Mind'

The tract which formed the opening salvo in the Oxford Movement campaign was privately circulated, as an anonymous publication, to potential clerical sympathisers in September 1833. The Irish Church Bill of 1833, proposing the suppression of certain bishoprics in Ireland provided its immediate occasion but Newman's approach indicates

concerns wider and deeper than the preservation of the
Established Church. The conflicting voices of the Dissenting
sects, who were attracting a number of Anglican seceders in
search of greater apostolic purity, raised the problem of
spiritual authority in acute form as political disestablishment
threatened. Newman reminds his readers that the Anglican
Church provides such an authority and tradition in the
evidence of a direct descent from the Church of the Apostles
asserted in the Prayer Book's Ordination Service.

Now then let me come at once to the subject which
leads me to address you. Should the Government and
Country so far forget their God as to cast off the
Church, to deprive it of its temporal honours and
substance, *on what* will you rest the claim of respect and
attention which you make upon your flocks? Hitherto
you have been upheld by your birth, your education,
your wealth, your connections; should these secular
advantages cease, on what must CHRIST's Ministers
depend? Is not this a serious practical question? We
know how miserable is the state of religious bodies not
supported by the State. Look at the Dissenters on all
sides of you, and you will see at once that their
Ministers, depending simply upon the people, become
the *creatures* of the people. Are you content that this
should be your case? Alas! can a greater evil befall
Christians than for their teachers to be guided by them,
instead of guiding? How can we 'hold fast the form of
sound words,' and 'keep that which is committed to our
trust,' if our influence is to depend simply on our
popularity? Is it not our very office to *oppose* the
world? can we then allow ourselves to *court* it? to
preach smooth things and prophesy deceits? to make
the way of life easy to the rich and indolent, and to bribe
the humbler classes by excitements and strong
intoxicating doctrine? Surely it must not be so; – and
the question recurs, on *what* are we to rest our
authority when the State deserts us?
CHRIST has not left His Church without claim of its
own upon the attention of men. Surely not. Hard

Master He cannot be, to bid us oppose the world, yet give us no credentials for so doing. There are some who rest their divine mission on their own unsupported assertion; others, who rest it upon their popularity; others, on their success; and others, who rest it upon their temporal distinctions. This last case has, perhaps, been too much our own; I fear we have neglected the real ground on which our authority is built, – OUR APOSTOLICAL DESCENT.

We have been born, not of blood, nor of the will of the flesh, nor of the will of man, but of God. The Lord JESUS CHRIST gave His Spirit to His Apostles; they in turn laid their hands on those who should succeed them; and these again on others; and so the sacred gift has been handed down to our present Bishops, who have appointed us as their assistants, and in some sense representatives.

Now every one of us believes this. I know that some will at first deny they do; still they do believe it. Only, it is not sufficiently practically impressed on their minds. They *do* believe it; for it is the doctrine of the Ordination Service, which they have recognised as truth in the most solemn season of their lives. In order, then, not to prove, but to remind and impress, I entreat your attention to the words used when you were made Minister of CHRIST's Church.

J.H. Newman, *Thoughts on the Ministerial Commission, Respectfully Addressed to the Clergy* (1833), pp.1-2.

The veiled challenge to believe or secede contained in his claim that the clergy *do* (or must) believe this was to be the root of much theological dispute and agonised soul-searching as unthinking compliance gave way to the strenuous effort to discover the precise implications of this belief.

The contributors to the Tracts and their disciples were variously nicknamed the Tractarians, the Oxford Movement or 'Puseyites'. This last sobriquet derived from the name of the movement's most socially and academically prestigious member who initialled his first contribution to the hitherto anonymous Tract series. Like Newman, Pusey insisted that beliefs must affect the life and form a reverential temper of mind, not just remain as cold intellectual propositions.

"It is difficult to say what people mean when they designate a class of views by my name; for since they are no peculiar doctrines, but it is rather a temper of mind which is so designated, it will vary according to the individual who uses it. Generally speaking, what is so designated may be reduced under the following heads; and what people mean to blame is what to them appears an excess of them.

(1) High thoughts of the two Sacraments.

(2) High estimate of Episcopacy as God's ordinance.

(3) High estimate of the visible Church as the Body wherein we are made and continue to be members of Christ.

(4) Regard for ordinances, as directing our devotions and disciplining us, such as daily public prayers, fasts and feasts, etc.

(5) Regard for the visible part of devotion, such as the decoration of the house of God, which acts insensibly on the mind.

(6) Reverence for and deference to the ancient Church, of which our own Church is looked upon as the representative to us, and by whose views and doctrines we interpret our own Church when her meaning is questioned or doubtful; in a word, reference to the ancient Church, instead of the Reformers, as the ultimate expounder of the meaning of our Church."

Quoted by H.P. Liddon in *Life of Edward
Bouverie Pusey* (1893–97), Vol. II, p.140.

Pusey's remarks underline the radical conservatism of Tractarianism's inspiration. His opening comment repudiates the charge of doctrinal innovation and his careful wording of the various headings emphasises that this is only a new way of seeing old truths, of restoring to established doctrines the pious attention they commanded in their earliest days. Central to this summary is the supremacy of the Church Visible, an order instituted by Christ and His Apostles, over the Church Invisible of all true believers, bound by a justifying faith and holding forms and ordinances as useful emblems, not necessarily channels for God's grace. Since the Anglican Church could only assure continued doctrinal purity by reference to the practices of the undivided Church of Antiquity, the Tractarians sought to emphasise the possibility of interpreting the doctrines embedded in the Prayer Book in a Catholic manner despite the Protestant intentions of their Reforming framers.

If the Church had a meaning and significance altogether more specific to a Tractarian than an Evangelical, so did the concept of Faith. Newman's Tract 73 'The Rationalistic and the Catholic Spirit Compared' recalls his article in the *British Critic* (see pp.6–8) in its distrust of the Evangelicals' 'justifying faith' whose presence is only to be divined by self-examination. Instead the Tractarians sought an authority transcending the capacity of individual minds which would also serve to counteract the prevailing atmosphere of rationalism.

Rationalism then in fact is a forgetfulness of GOD's power, disbelief of the existence of a First Cause sufficient to account for any events or facts, however marvellous or extraordinary, and a consequent measuring of the credibility of things, not by the power and other attributes of GOD, but by our own knowledge; a limiting the possible to the actual, and denying the indefinite range of GOD's operations beyond our means of apprehending them. . . . Instead of looking out of ourselves, and trying to catch glimpses of GOD's workings, from any quarter, – throwing ourselves forward upon Him and waiting on Him, we sit at home bringing everything to ourselves, enthroning ourselves as the centre of all things, and refusing to believe any thing that does not force itself upon our minds as true. Our private judgment is made every thing to us, – is contemplated, recognized, and referred to as the arbiter of all questions, and as independent of every thing external to us. Nothing is considered to have an existence except so far forth as our minds discern it. The notion of half views and partial knowledge, of guesses, surmises, hopes and fears, of truths faintly apprehended and not understood, of isolated facts in the great scheme of providence, in a word, of Mystery, is discarded. Hence a distinction is drawn between what is called Objective and Subjective Truth, and Religion is said to consist in a reception of the latter. . . . In short, he [the rationalist] owns that faith, viewed with reference to its objects, is never more than an opinion, and is pleasing to GOD, not as an active principle apprehending different doctrines, but as a result and fruit, and therefore an evidence of past diligence, independent inquiry, dispassionateness, and the like. Rationalism takes the words of Scripture as signs of Ideas; Faith, of Things or Realities.

J.H. Newman, *Tract 73* (1836), pp.3–5.

Rationalism makes man the measure of God and so sees in Scripture the records of more primitive minds from which later eras of progress could extract still acceptable ideas whilst discarding the credulous accounts of miracles and wonders. For the Tractarians God's sublimity lay in the very fact of His mysteriousness. Being transcendent God could not, as eighteenth-century rationalists claimed, be deduced from His creation but he could be glimpsed by the eyes of faith as objectively present in it.

The distinction made in Newman's final sentence informs the following poem by Keble. Before the Oxford Movement as such was born Keble had published *The Christian Year*, a series of hymns arranged around the calendar of the Church's year. George Herbert's poetry convinced Keble that this form might be used within the Anglican tradition to combine worship and instruction. Yet so attached in the popular mind had hymn-singing and Dissent become that Keble's disciple, Hurrell Froude, feared lest men might take him for a Methodist on account of this publication.

THERE is a book, who runs may read,
    Which heavenly truth imparts,
And all the lore its scholars need,
    Pure eyes and Christian hearts.

The works of God above, below,
    Within us and around,
Are pages in that book, to show
    How God Himself is found.

The glorious sky embracing all
    Is like the Maker's love,
Wherewith encompass'd, great and small
    In peace and order move.

The Moon above, the Church below,
    A wondrous race they run,
But all their radiance, all their glow,
    Each borrows of its Sun.

        *   *   *

The dew of Heaven is like Thy grace,
    It steals in silence down;
But where it lights, the favour'd place
    By richest fruits is known.

One Name above all glorious names
    With its ten thousand tongues
The everlasting sea proclaims,
    Echoing angelic songs.

The raging Fire, the roaring Wind,
    Thy boundless power display:
But in the gentler breeze we find
    Thy Spirit's viewless way.

Two worlds are ours: 'tis only Sin
    Forbids us to descry
The mystic heaven and earth within,
    Plain as the sea and sky.

Thou, who hast given me eyes to see
And love this sight so fair,
Give me a heart to find out Thee,
And read Thee everywhere.

J. Keble, 'Septuagesima Sunday', vv.1-4; 8-12 in
The Christian Year (1827).

Implicit in this poem are the emphases on sacramentalism and reserve in communicating religious knowledge that Keble imparted to Tractarianism. Nature did not present a series of proofs for God's existence, but rather, God, being greater than His creation, spoke through nature to convey something of His presence by sign and symbol. God is not to be deduced by logic but reveals His mysteries by glimpses whose significance becomes comprehensible only to the eyes of the faithful who bring 'pure eyes and Christian hearts'. Keble's choice of natural symbolism in the poem is not a matter of analogy but indicative of his perception of humanity as an organic part of God's creation. In this framework Christian works can be seen not as useful evidence of salvation but as an integral part of God's plan where the seed of grace alighting on 'the favour'd place / By richest fruit is known'.

The Life of Devotion

A sermon preached by Pusey, to commemorate the consecration of the church he had anonymously financed, swiftly discountenances two popular misconceptions about the Oxford Movement. First, for its founders, the Oxford Movement's concern with the 'beauty of holiness' was not a matter of externals but of a disciplined inner life of penitence and sanctification, which alone could inculcate the humility necessary to preserve the wonder of God's condescension to man. Secondly Pusey's benefaction to Leeds demonstrates that, although propagated in a university environment, the Oxford Movement's lasting contribution to Anglican life was devotional rather than theological. Pusey, often seen as the most scholarly and remote of the founders, exercised influence far beyond Oxford through his former pupils and disciples. He was instrumental in the establishment of Anglican sisterhoods and semi-monastic communities who exercised their 'care of souls' around the life of new churches in areas of acute urban deprivation.

And to this end, of fixing our purpose of more stedfast warfare under Christ's banner, it may by His gracious aid be of some help, now at the close, to name some few simple rules, familiar perhaps to many of you, which yet to some, who are beginners, may be useful. And yet, if any have not begun to live under rule, burden yourselves not with too much at once, lest it oppress or weary you, or you tire after a time, or it become mechanical, and you become distracted by thinking of your rules rather than of Him, under Whom you would thereby bring yourself under rule, Whose Holy Will you wish to make your Rule.

Above all, whatever you attempt, impress on the mind and pray God there to write a deep consciousness of your own helplessness and inability to begin or continue or hold on in any good. And this, not in the way of formal acknowledgment, (for this, all ever make,) but impressing it and stamping it upon your inward souls, and acting upon it, whatever else you are doing, in continual, quick, instantaneous prayer for the aid of God. This very habit itself plainly cannot be gained at once. For, gained, it is to live in heaven, in continual intercourse with God; we ever breathing up to God and in God, His pity ever descending upon us. It too must be His gift; as, when it is given, it is the key to all His other gifts, and the treasures of His love. Yet this too He will bestow upon us, in degrees, as we use faithfully His secret drawings to look up to Him.

But, first, in order of time, will perhaps be that searching of the heart, whereof I have so often spoken, both in order to gain a clean heart, by pouring out our whole selves in penitent confession to God, and also to know more clearly, what are our chief enemies. And these, indeed, we cannot expect to know all at once, as neither can we all our past sins. The eye must be cleansed, in order fully to behold sin, as well as to see God. . . .

And as we make progress in our spiritual conflict, we shall see what occasions are most hurtful to us, in what way our sin most steals upon us or assails us; and so we can either by ourselves, or by help of some who has the care of human souls, form rules to ourselves, how we can keep off the occasion, or be strengthened under it. For to come into temptation with no fixed rule to guide us, nothing to appeal to against our biassed judgment, is to give ourselves over to defeat.

E.B. Pusey, *A Course of Sermons on Solemn Subjects delivered at St. Saviour's Leeds* (1845), pp.343-45; 347.

Submission and obedience practised amidst the demands and irritations of daily domestic life are the two Christian virtues most frequently praised in the works of the Anglo-Catholic novelist, Charlotte Yonge. She herself was in the habit of submitting her manuscripts to John Keble, her local parson, for his approval. Authority, to which the Oxford Movement had appealed, is invested in this passage first in the Church and Prayer Book, then in the voice of an experienced Christian adult. The finely-strung consciences of adolescents in Yonge's novels act as evidence of the importance of reserve in communicating religious knowledge. Humility, which comes from a realisation of their inexperience, the importance of a 'right heart' and an awed seriousness underlie Ethel and Meta's conversation.

'We have learnt so much lately about self-denial, and crossing one's own inclinations, and enduring hardness. And here I live with two dear kind people, who only try to keep every little annoyance from my path. I can't wish for a thing without getting it – I am waited on all day long, and I feel like one of the women that are at ease – one of the careless daughters.'

'I think still papa would say it was your happy contented temper that made you find no vexation.'

'But that sort of temper is not goodness. I was born with it; I never did mind anything, not even being punished, they say, unless I knew papa was grieved, which always did make me unhappy enough. I laughed, and went to play most saucily, whatever they did to me. If I had striven for the temper, it would be worth having, but it is my nature. And, Ethel,' she added, in a low voice, as the tears came into her eyes, 'don't you remember last Sunday? I felt myself so vain and petted a thing! as if I had no share in the Cup of suffering, and did not deserve to call myself a member – it seemed ungrateful.'

Ethel felt ashamed, as she heard of warmer feelings than her own had been, expressed in that lowered trembling voice, and she sought for the answer that would only come to her mind in sense, not at first in words. 'Discipline,' said she, 'would not that show the willingness to have the part? Taking the right times for refusing oneself some pleasant thing.'

'Would not that be only making up something for oneself?' said Meta.

'No, the Church orders it. It is in the Prayer-book,' said Ethel. 'I mean one can do little secret things – not read storybooks on those days, or keep some tiresome sort of work for them. It is very trumpery, but it keeps the remembrance, and it is not so much as if one did not heed.'

'I'll think,' said Meta, sighing. 'If only I felt myself at work, not to please myself, but to be of use. Ha!' she cried, springing up, 'I do believe I see Dr. May coming!'

'Let us run and meet him,' said Ethel.

They did so, and he called out his wishes of many happy returns of blithe days to the little birthday queen, then added, 'You both look grave, though – have they deserted you?'

'No, papa, we have been having a talk,' said Ethel. 'May I tell him, Meta? I want to know what he says.'

Meta had not bargained for this, but she was very much in earnest, and there was nothing formidable in Dr. May, so she assented.

'Meta is longing to be at work – she thinks she is of no use,' said Ethel – 'she says she never does anything but please herself.'

'Pleasing oneself is not the same as trying to please oneself,' said Dr. May, kindly.

'And she thinks it cannot be safe or right,' added Ethel, 'to live that happy bright life, as if people without care or trouble could not be living as Christians are meant to live. Is that it, Meta?'

'Yes, I think it is,' said Meta. 'I seem to be only put here to be made much of !'

'What did David say, Meta?' returned Dr. May.

'My Shepherd is the living Lord,
    Nothing therefore I need:
In pastures fair, near pleasant streams,
    He setteth me to feed.'

'Then you think,' said Meta, much touched, 'that I ought to look on this as "the pastures fair," and be thankful. I hope I was not unthankful.'

'O, no,' said Ethel. 'It was the wish to bear hardness, and be a good soldier, was it not?'

'Ah! my dear,' he said, 'the rugged path and dark valley will come in His own fit time. . . .

Meta was much affected, and began to put together what the father and daughter had said. Perhaps the little modes of secret discipline, of which Ethel had spoken, might be the true means of clasping the staff – perhaps she had been impatient, and wanting in humility in craving for the strife, when her armour was scarce put on.

C. Yonge, *The Daisy Chain* (1856), Part I, Ch. 26.

Some women influenced by Tractarian ideals felt called to a more formal practice of life under the rule and the Protestant sisterhoods that Pusey had encouraged aroused the kind of deep suspicions which surface in the following fictional portrait of an English squire's daughter whose vocation is diagnosed as sanctified self-will.

Both she and the vicar had a great wish that she should lead a "devoted life;" but then they both disdained to use common means for their object. The good old English plan of district visiting, by which ladies can have mercy on the bodies and souls of those below them, without casting off the holy discipline which a home, even the most ungenial, alone supplies, savoured too much of mere "Protestantism." It might be God's plan for Christianizing England just now, but that was no reason, alas! for its being their plan: they wanted something more "Catholic," more in accordance with Church principles; (for, indeed, is it not the business of the Church to correct the errors of Providence?) and what they sought they found at once in a certain favourite establishment of the vicar's, a Church-of-England *béguinage*, or quasi-Protestant nunnery, which he fostered in a neighbouring city, and went thither on all high tides to confess the young ladies, who were in all things nuns, but bound by no vows, except, of course, such as they might choose to make for themselves in private.

Here they laboured among the lowest haunts of misery and sin, piously and self-denyingly enough, sweet souls! in hope of "the peculiar crown," and a higher place in heaven than the relations whom they had left behind them "in the world," and unshackled by the interference of parents, and other such merely fleshly relationships, which, as they cannot have been instituted by God merely to be trampled under foot on the path to holiness, and cannot well have instituted themselves . . ., must needs have been instituted by the devil. And so more than one girl in that nunnery, and out of it, too, believed in her inmost heart, though her "Catholic principles," by a happy inconsistency, forbade her to say so.

In a moment of excitement, fascinated by the romance of the notion, Argemone had proposed to her mother to allow her to enter this *béguinage*, and called in the vicar as advocate; which produced a correspondence between him and Mrs. Lavington,

stormy on her side, provokingly calm on his: and when
the poor lady, tired of raging, had descended to an
affecting appeal to his human sympathies, entreating
him to spare a mother's feelings, he had answered with
the same impassive fanaticism, that "he was surprised at
her putting a mother's selfish feelings in competition
with the sanctity of her child," and that "had his own
daughter shown such a desire for a higher vocation, he
should have esteemed it the very highest honour;" to
which Mrs. Lavington answered, naïvely enough, that
"it depended very much on what his daughter was
like." – So he was all but forbidden the house.
Nevertheless he contrived, by means of this same secret
correspondence, to keep alive in Argemone's mind the
longing to turn nun, and fancied honestly that he was
doing God service, while he was pampering the poor
girl's lust for singularity and self-glorification.

C. Kingsley, Yeast (1848), Ch. 10.

The good work done by such groups in slum areas is not in
question (Argemone finally dies of typhus contracted in the
slums) but the motivation is. Protestant sisterhoods were, for
Kingsley, a contradiction in terms. Roman Catholic nunneries
at least live in subjection to an agreed rule, but, by virtue of
their Protestantism, Anglican sisterhoods must foster spiritual
pride and disobedience masquerading as self-sacrifice.
Kingsley's outspoken nature never comprehended the
Tractarian doctrine of Reserve and he is happy to join forces
with popular Protestantism in denouncing it as an inclination
for the clandestine. *Yeast* also wages war on a wider front
against Tractarianism's influence. Whilst admitting the moral
seriousness it had awakened in cultivated circles, Kingsley
dismisses its socio-political concomitant, the paternalist
economics and neo-medievalism of the Tory Young England
Movement, as anachronistic. Other Tractarian-encouraged
errors and vices denounced are the nursing of the impulse to
secede to Rome, Mariolatry, uncritical adulation of the Early
Church, unmanliness and unEnglishness.

Trollope's deep-seated antipathy to Evangelicalism renders

him more sympathetic than Kingsley to the Oxford Movement, yet the following passage from *Barchester Towers*, in which the attractive Mr Arabin's emergence as Tractarian champion is described, also reflects many of the popular prejudices against the Oxford Movement. A perverse desire for self-martyrdom, Newman-worship, hankering after Roman ritual, a yearning for certainty, an intellectual disdain for the humdrum toil of parochial clergy all need to be set right by the stout moral example of Protestant endeavour.

Mr. Arabin was ordained, and became a fellow soon after taking his degree, and shortly after that was chosen professor of poetry.

And now came the moment of his great danger. After many mental struggles, and an agony of doubt which may be well surmised, the great prophet of the Tractarians confessed himself a Roman Catholic. Mr. Newman left the Church of England, and with him carried many a waverer. He did not carry off Mr. Arabin, but the escape which that gentleman had was a very narrow one. He left Oxford for a while that he might meditate in complete peace on the step which appeared to him to be all but unavoidable, and shut himself up in a little village on the seashore of one of our remotest counties, that he might learn by communing with his own soul whether or no he could with a safe conscience remain within the pale of his Mother Church.

Things would have gone badly with him there had he been left entirely to himself. Everything was against him: all his worldly interests required him to remain a Protestant; and he looked on his worldly interests as a legion of foes, to get the better of whom was a point of extremest honour. In his then state of ecstatic agony such a conquest would have cost him little; he could easily have thrown away all his livelihood: but it cost him much to get over the idea that by choosing the Church of England he should be open in his own mind to the charge that he had been led to such a choice by unworthy motives. Then his heart was against him; he loved with a strong and eager love the man who had hitherto been his guide, and yearned to follow his footsteps. His tastes were against him: the ceremonies and pomps of the Church of Rome, their august feasts and solemn fasts, invited his imagination and pleased his eye. His flesh was against him: how great an aid it would be to a poor, weak, wavering man to be constrained to high moral duties, self-denial, obedience and chastity by laws which were certain in their enactments, and not to be broken without loud, palpable, unmistakable sin! Then his faith was against him: he required to believe so much; panted so eagerly to give signs of his belief; deemed it so insufficient to wash himself simply in the waters of Jordan; that some great deed, such as that of forsaking everything for a true church, had for him allurements almost past withstanding.

Mr. Arabin was at this time a very young man, and when he left Oxford for his far retreat was much too confident in his powers of fence, and too apt to look down on the ordinary sense of ordinary people, to expect aid in the battle that he had to fight from any chance inhabitants of the spot which he had selected. But Providence was good to him; and there, in that all but desolate place, on the storm-beat shore of that distant sea he met one who gradually calmed his mind, quieted his imagination, and taught him something of a Christian's duty. When Mr. Arabin left Oxford, he was inclined to look upon the rural clergymen of most English parishes almost with contempt. It was his ambition, should he remain within the fold of their church, to do somewhat towards redeeming and rectifying their inferiority, and to assist in infusing energy and faith into the hearts of Christian ministers, who were, as he thought, too often satisfied to go through life without much show of either.

And yet it was from such a one that Mr. Arabin in his extremest need received that aid which he so much required. It was from the poor curate of a small Cornish parish that he first learnt to know that the highest laws for the governance of a Christian's duty must act from within and not from without; that no man can become a serviceable servant solely by obedience to written edicts; and that the safety which he was about to seek within the gates of Rome was no other than the selfish freedom from personal danger which the bad soldier attempts to gain who counterfeits illness on the eve of battle.

A. Trollope, *Barchester Towers* (1857), Ch. 20.

Mr Arabin is introduced to the world of ecclesiastical politics as a weapon of which a wily old-fashioned High Churchman might avail himself to counteract Evangelicalism rampant in the person of the Bishop and his chaplain, Mr Slope (see pp.10–11). Historically speaking, although the Oxford Professorship of Poetry had at one time appeared to have become a Tractarian stronghold, it is highly improbable that a Tractarian such as Arabin would have been appointed Dean in the 1850s. Prime Minister Palmerston's bishop-maker, his Evangelical stepson-in-law, Lord Shaftesbury, worked hard to ensure Evangelical supremacy and combat Tractarian influence.

Newman's secession to Rome was insufficient to dampen the enthusiasm of some of the Movement's younger disciples. Mark Pattison, son of an Evangelical parson and later contributor to the Broad Church *Essays and Reviews* (see pp.65–66), fell under Newman's spell as an undergraduate and remained a devotee of the Oxford Movement even after Newman departed in 1845. He was an active contributor to Tractarian projects such as the series of *Lives of the English Saints*. The diary entry recording his visit to Newman's retreat at Littlemore reveals both the formal regimen observed in the semi-monastic community and something of the over-scrupulous moral temperature-taking practised by young disciples.

On Saturday, 30th September 1843, I went by invitation on a short visit. The Diary is as follows:–

"Newman kinder, but not perfectly so. Vespers at eight. Compline at nine. How low, mean, selfish, my mind has been to-day; all my good seeds vanished; grovelling, sensual, animalish; I am not indeed worthy to come under this roof.

"Sunday, October 1. – St. John called me at 5.30, and at 6 went to Matins, which with Lauds and Prime take about an hour and a half; afterwards returned to my room and prayed, with some effect, I think. Tierce at 9, and at 11 to church, – communion. More attentive and devout than I have been for some time; hope I am coming into a better frame; 37 communicants. Returned and had ✳ ✳ ✳ breakfast. Had some discomfort at waiting for food so long, which I have not done since I have been unwell this summer, but struggled against it, and in some degree threw it off. Walked up and down with St. John in the garden; Newman afterwards joined us."

M. Pattison, *Memoirs* (1885), pp.190-91.

Pattison's emergence as a celebrated student of Aristotelian logic and his increasing interest in German scholarship subsequently led him to detect a blinkered narrowness in the Tractarian position.

I venerated Newman himself as having been so much to me in so many ways; and I had too little knowledge to see how limited his philosophical acquirements were. The force of his dialectic, and the beauty of his rhetorical exposition were such that one's eye and ear were charmed, and one never thought of inquiring on how narrow a basis of philosophical culture his great gifts were expended. A. P. Stanley once said to me, "How different the fortunes of the Church of England might have been if Newman had been able to read German." That puts the matter in a nut-shell; Newman assumed and adorned the narrow basis on which Laud had stood 200 years before. All the grand development of human reason, from Aristotle down to Hegel, was a sealed book to him.

Ibid, p.210.

Ritualist Theology and Practice

The early Tractarians rightly repudiated Ritualist excesses as a necessary concomitant of their theology but it is easy to see how an enthusiasm for ceremony and symbol could be derived from their teaching. The conception of the two sacraments rather than the preaching of the Word as central to worship, the notion of the Visible Church as a divinely appointed order and the significance of church buildings as contributory to sacramental worship in conjunction with the opportunities offered by the building of new churches all helped to focus attention on liturgy and ritual. This passage by Purchas, whose name was to be enshrined in a Privy Council Judgement of 1871 concerning practices compatible with Anglicanism, provides a concise explanation of the theology of Ritualism.

> Every part of the Church must have a ritual, and as there is but one Catholic Church, so the ritual of every portion thereof will have a family likeness, and be one in spirit though diverse in details. Ritual and Ceremonial are the hieroglyphics of the Catholic religion, a language understanded of the faithful, a kind of parable in action, for as of old when He walked the earth, our blessed Lord, still present in His divine and human nature in the Holy Eucharist on the altars of His Church, still spiritually present at the Common Prayers, does not speak unto us 'without a parable'. But as our Lord's 'visage was marred more than any man, and His form more than the sons of men', so has it fared, at least in His Church in this land, with the aspect of His worship on earth. For the last three hundred years, brief but brilliant periods excepted, our ritual has lost all unity of significance of expression. We have treated 'The Book of Common Prayer and Administration of the Sacraments, and other Rites and Ceremonies of the Church' much as if it were simply a collection of sundry Forms of Prayer, overlooking the fact that besides these there are acts to be done, and functions to be performed. And these have been done infrequently, not to say imperfectly.

The old Puritan idea of Divine Service is confession of sin, prayer to God and intercession for our wants, bodily and spiritual. Another theological school, more perhaps in vogue, looks upon praise as the great element of worship – praise, that is, apart from *Eucharistia*, itself, in one sense, a mighty Act of Praise. Hence one Priest with his form-of-prayer theory affects a bald, chilling, and apparently indevout worship, whilst another lavishes all the splendour of his ritual upon his forms of prayer which are said in choir; and both depress, by defective teaching and a maimed ritual, the distinctive service of Christianity. Matins and Evensong are performed with a severe simplicity by the one, in an ornate manner by the other. Both schools have elements of truth in them, both err after the same manner, viz. in undue exaltation of the Church's ordinary Office, and in depreciation of the Sacramental system – at least the celebration of the Holy Eucharist is not with them the centre of Christian Worship. Yet surely the Communion Service is something more than a mere form of prayer in the opinion of even the laxest school of theology.

J. Purchas, *The Directorium Anglicanum* (1858), pp.vii-viii.

The conscious archaisms (for ease of comprehension I have deleted the copious 'ſ 's for 's's with which Purchas sprinkled his text and the marginal comments in the style of Prayer Book rubrics) denote Ritualism's real debt to Victorian neo-medievalism despite their claim to derive their practices from those of the Ancient Church.

A useful checklist of the mannerisms and sillier excesses of younger Tractarians appears in an essay by William John Conybeare which deserves to be better known, not only on account of its contemporary notoriety, but because its attempt to classify the subdivisions of the various strands of Anglicanism and its methods of quantifying party support were adopted as the basis for many subsequent assessments.

Who does not recognise, when he meets them in the railway or the street, the clipped shirt-collar, the stiff and tie-less neckcloth, the M.B. coat and cassock waistcoat, the cropped hair and un-whiskered cheek? Who does not know that the wearer of this costume, will talk of 'the Holy Altar,' and 'the Blessed Virgin,' of 'Saint Ignatius Loyola,' and 'Saint Alphonso de Liguori?' And that he will date his letters on 'the eve of St. Chad,' or 'the Morrow of St. Martin?' Who has not seen the youthful Presbyter bowing to the altar, and turning his back on the people? Who has not heard him intoning the prayers, and preaching in his surplice on the 'holy obedience,' due from laity to priesthood? Who is ignorant that he reads the offertory after his sermon, and sends round little bags at the end of long poles, which are thrust in the faces of the worshippers to extort their contributions? Who has not noticed the gaudy furniture of his church, the tippeted altar, the candles blazing at noon-day, the wreaths of flowers changing their colour with feast or fast, the medieval emblems embroidered on the altar-cloth? After all, these are but the harmless fopperies, only mischievous if they stir up the wrath of the people. But the Tractarian mode of celebrating the Communion deserves graver censure.

W.J. Conybeare, 'Church Parties', *Edinburgh Review*, Vol. 98 (1853), p.315.

The continuous thread of clothing imagery helps to support the air of self-admiring foppery Conybeare wishes to lend their attention to externals. The nickname for those hallmarks of Tractarian clerical attire, the Mark of the Beast long black frock coat and cassock waistcoat, allegedly originated in tailor's shorthand.

Some readers have felt that Tennyson used his Arthurian sources to produce the great apologia for Protestant manhood and Victorian family life in his *Idylls of the King*. The life embraced by Arthur's rival King Pellam carried an unmistakable warning against the excesses of second-generation Tractarianism. His morbid preoccupation with fasting, celibacy, relic worship and superstition, unhealthy in themselves, are also shown to be deeply unpatriotic in that they

were adopted in rivalry to Arthur's successful Protestant rule.
Pellam's reliance upon legend as the basis for his appeal to a
greater apostolic purity outrages by its impudence and reflects
popular scepticism at the Tractarian enthusiasm for
republishing the legends of the Early Church. The appeal of
the celibate life is repeatedly revealed in the *Idylls* as the reverse
side of the adulterous desires of Lancelot and Guinevere. Both
threaten the very foundation of society and social
responsibility. Tennyson's diction contrives to convict Pellam
of unmanly rudeness, spiritual arrogance and inner collapse.

> 'Sir King' they brought report 'we hardly found,
> So bushed about it is with gloom, the hall
> Of him to whom ye sent us, Pellam, once
> A Christless foe of thine as ever dashed
> Horse against horse; but seeing that thy realm
> Hath prospered in the name of Christ, the King
> Took, as in rival heat, to holy things;
> And finds himself descended from the Saint
> Arimathæan Joseph; him who first
> Brought the great faith to Britain over seas;
> He boasts his life as purer than thine own;
> Eats scarce enow to keep his pulse abeat;
> Hath pushed aside his faithful wife, nor lets
> Or dame or damsel enter at his gates
> Lest he should be polluted. This gray King
> Showed us a shrine wherein were wonders – yea –
> Rich arks with priceless bones of martyrdom,
> Thorns of the crown and shivers of the cross,
> And therewithal (for thus he told us) brought
> By holy Joseph hither, that same spear
> Wherewith the Roman pierced the side of Christ.
> He much amazed us; after, when we sought
> The tribute, answered "I have quite foregone
> All matters of this world: Garlon, mine heir,
> Of him demand it," which this Garlon gave
> With much ado, railing at thine and thee.

> Lord Tennyson, 'Balin and Balan', ll.91-116 in
> *Idylls of the King* (1885).

Two Facets of the Catholic Tradition

Liberal Catholicism

Given the antithesis between faith and reason so strongly stressed by the originators of the Oxford Movement, the outcry caused in Anglo-Catholic circles by the appearance of *Lux Mundi* (1889) should not surprise us. Criticism focused on the essay by Charles Gore, Principal of Pusey House, Oxford. Pursuing his vision of a 'Liberal Catholicism', Gore attempted to relate Catholic dogma to the theological implications of recent historical and scientific criticism, seen in the work of the Broad Church's contribution to *Essays and Reviews* (see pp.65–66). Gore stands firmly in the Tractarian tradition in emphasising the role of the Church in interpreting Scripture but allows for the contribution to be made by what Newman comprehensively dismissed as 'subjective' considerations. A refusal to accept an evolutionary view of inspiration, he warned, would ensure the rapid death in a theological backwater of the Catholic tradition he earnestly desired to perpetuate.

> Hitherto nothing has been said about that part of the Holy Spirit's work which is called the inspiration of Scripture. It has been kept to the last because of the great importance of putting it in context with less familiar truths. The Scriptures have, it is a commonplace to say, suffered greatly from being isolated. This is as true whether we are considering them as a source of evidence or as the sphere of inspiration.
>
> As a source of evidence they contain the record of historical facts with some of which at any rate the Creed of Christendom is inseparably interwoven. Thus it is impossible for Christians who know what they are about, to under-estimate the importance of the historical evidence for those facts at least of which the Creed contains a summary. But the tendency with books of historical evidence has been, at least till recently, to exaggerate the extent to which the mere

evidence of remote facts can compel belief. . . . In order to have grounds for believing the facts, in order to be susceptible of their evidence, we require an antecedent state of conception and expectation. A whole set of presuppositions about God, about the slavery of sin, about the reasonableness of redemption, must be present with us. So only can the facts presented to us in the Gospel come to us as credible things, or as parts of an intelligible universe, correlated elements in a rational whole. Now the work of the Spirit in the Church has been to keep alive and real these presuppositions, this frame of mind. He convinces of sin, of righteousness, of judgment. He does this not merely in isolated individuals however numerous, but in an organized continuous society. The spiritual life of the Church assures me that in desiring union with God, in feeling the burden of sin, in hungering for redemption, I am not doing an eccentric, abnormal thing. I am doing only what belongs to the best and richest movement of humanity. More than this, it assures me that assent to the claims and promises of Jesus Christ satisfies these spiritual needs in such a way as to produce the strongest, the most lasting, the most catholic sort of human character. The historical life of the Church thus in every age 'setting to its seal' that God's offer in Christ is true, reproduces the original 'witness,' commends it to conscience and reason, spans the gulf of the ages, and brings down remote and alien incidents into close and intelligible familiarity. . . .

Once again: an enlarged study of comparative history has led to our perceiving that the various sorts of mental or literary activity develop in their different lines out of an earlier condition in which they lie fused and undifferentiated. This we can vaguely call the mythical stage of mental evolution. A myth is not a falsehood; it is a product of mental activity, as instructive and rich as any later product, but its characteristic is that it is not yet distinguished into history, and poetry, and philosophy. It is all of these in the germ, as dream and imagination, and thought and experience, are fused in the mental furniture of a child's mind. 'These myths or current stories,' says Grote writing of Greek history, 'the spontaneous and earliest growth of the Greek mind, constituted at the same time the entire intellectual stock of the age to which they belonged. They are the common root of all those different ramifications into which the mental activity of the Greeks subsequently diverged; containing as it were the preface and germ of the positive history and philosophy, the dogmatic theology and the professed romance, which we shall hereafter trace, each in its separate development.' Now has the Jewish history such earlier stage: does it pass back out of history into myth? In particular, are not its earlier narratives, before the call of Abraham, of the nature of myth, in which we cannot distinguish the historical germ, though we do not at all deny that it exists? The inspiration of these narratives is as conspicuous as that of any part of Scripture, but is there anything to prevent our regarding these great inspirations about the origin of all things, – the nature of sin, the judgment of God on sin, and the alienation among men which follows their alienation from God, – as conveyed to us in that form of myth or allegorical picture, which is the earliest mode in which the mind of man apprehended truth?

The present writer, believing that the modern development of historical criticism is reaching results as sure, where it is fairly used, as scientific inquiry, and feeling therefore that the warning which the name of Galileo must ever bring before the memory of churchmen, is not unneeded now, believes also that the Church is in no way restrained from admitting the modifications just hinted at, in what has latterly been the current idea of inspiration.

'The Holy Spirit and Inspiration', *Lux Mundi*, ed.
C. Gore (1889), pp.337-38; 356-57.

Inscape

Gerard Manley Hopkins' struggle to reconcile his enjoyment of nature and his poetic gift with the self-disciplined, sacrificial life of the Jesuit priest is well-known. Though his veneration for the Visible Church never seems to have equalled that of the Tractarians, much of his poetic theory and practice shows the mark of the sacramental and penitential teaching he would have received from Pusey who had been his spiritual adviser as an undergraduate.

The sonnet below reveals Hopkins' sacramental enjoyment of nature particularly clearly as the final lines, leading to a vision of the indwelling presence of God in the distinctive form and pattern of the night sky, articulate his theory of 'inscape'.

> Look at the stars! look, look up at the skies!
> O look at all the fire-folk sitting in the air!
> The bright boroughs, the circle-citadels there!
> Down in dim woods the diamond delves! the elves'-
>   eyes!
> The grey lawns cold where gold, where quickgold lies!
> Wind-beat whitebeam! airy abeles set on a flare!
> Flake-doves sent floating forth at a farmyard scare! –
> A well! it is all a purchase, all is a prize.
>
> Buy them! bid then! – What? – Prayer, patience, alms,
>   vows.
> Look, look: a May-mess, like on orchard boughs!
> Look! March-bloom, like on mealed-with-yellow
>   sallows!
> These are indeed the barn; withindoors house
> The shocks. This piece-bright paling shuts the spouse
>   Christ home, Christ and his mother and all his
>   hallows.
>
>   G.M. Hopkins, 'The Starlight Night' (1877).

The notion of a vision only to be attained by a disciplined inner life of prayer, patience, alms and vows would surely have found favour with Pusey.

The form of the poem reflects this idea. The exuberant moment of wonder, heard in ejaculatory phrases and invitation, is achieved only at the expense of a carefully wrought, highly-disciplined inner structure. Hopkins' isolation from a reading public, though emotionally searing, encouraged his revolutionary techniques; yet this sonnet reveals an understanding shared with the Tractarians of 'a doctrine lying hid in language'.

3 The Broad Church

The phrase 'Broad Church' usefully indicates the latitude necessary to produce any defining limits which might satisfactorily embrace Thomas Arnold, Maurice, Jowett and Stanley. Dr Arnold indeed strictly predates the popular mid-century use of the term but by many of the next generation he was seen as a progenitor of the liberalising school. Coleridge's place is harder still to define, since his anti-rationalist bias and emphasis on the Bible as confirmatory of belief rather than its sole source might seem to entitle him to a position in the ranks of those who influenced the thought of the Oxford Movement. Yet Stanley (see pp.68–70) claims him, on the grounds of his 'Germanising influence' alone, as responsible for the theological atmosphere which made the Broad Church *Essays and Reviews* both possible and inevitable. In effect the figures included in this chapter all wished to emend the orthodox limits of Anglicanism in different ways.

Arnold and Stanley strove for a National Church which should be inclusive rather than exclusive. The state would act as a guarantor of religious freedom whilst the Anglican heritage would counteract the potential excesses of individualistic Nonconformity. For these two men dogmatic precision paled in significance beside the search for unity.

Jowett and his fellow essayists shared the view that to retreat from the threat of German criticism and retire behind the fence of orthodox assertions of the faith could only preserve an ossified dogma. They were concerned to allow the fruits of Biblical and historical criticism within the Anglican palisade but on their own terms, accommodating criticism to belief rather than discarding belief for rationalism. As a believer with unorthodox views Maurice finds a niche in this section, although the importance he attached to his work as a theologian distinguishes him from the liberal anti-dogmatism of these other Broad Churchmen.

Although two major strands of Broad Church concern emerge – concern with the concept of the Church and receptivity of liberal criticism – the heterodox position adopted by these men dictates the arrangement of this chapter largely in terms of individuals rather than by topic. One common characteristic illuminated the lives and work of all these men – a strong moral feeling which showed itself in concern for the social and educational welfare of an avowedly Christian nation.

The literary texts I have chosen, whether inspired by liberalising tendencies or a criticism of them, reflect something of the problem with which thinking men were faced. Whilst a series of legal cases established in piecemeal fashion views that were not incompatible with a profession of Anglicanism, how far could the process of jettisoning the old dogmatic certainties go without religion becoming merely a matter of moral sentiment?

Coleridge – A Broad Church Forebear?

Any attempt to represent Coleridge's thinking on matters religious and theological is bedevilled by the fragmentary, unsystematic nature of his writings. The following extracts aim rather to suggest a few strands of his thoughts which fed into the later Broad Church patterns of faith and practice. Reacting against the rationalist bias of eighteenth-century theology, which often sought to deduce God from the evidences of nature and against the appeal to feeling alone, Coleridge emphasises the importance of the will, the conscience and experience in confirming the truths of Christianity.

> He, who begins by loving Christianity better than Truth, will proceed by loving his own Sect or Church better than Christianity, and end in loving himself better than all. ... The following may, I think, be taken as a safe and useful Rule in religious inquiries. Ideas, that derive their origin and substance from the *Moral* Being, and to the reception of which as true *objectively* (that is, as corresponding to a *reality* out of

> the human mind) we are determined by a *practical*
> interest exclusively, may not, like theoretical or
> speculative Positions, be pressed onward into all their
> possible *logical* consequences. . . . Christianity is not a
> Theory, or a Speculation; but a *Life*; – not a *Philosophy*
> of Life, but a Life and a living Process. . . . TRY IT.
>
> S.T. Coleridge, *Aids to Reflection* (1825), pp.66;
> 108; 134.

Alive to German Biblical scholarship, Coleridge anticipated
the difficulties which would arise from a dogged clinging to
theories of plenary inspiration (the belief that the Bible not
only contained but was in every part the Word of God) and
literal interpretation. Such historical obscurantism in fact
lessens the Bible's real function as a revelation for all men and
all times, confirming and extending the experiences of the
believer.

> I take up this work [the Bible] with the purpose to read
> it for the first time as I should read any other work, – as
> far at least as I can or dare. . . . And need I say that I
> have met every where more or less copious sources of
> truth, and power, and purifying impulses; – that I have
> found words for my inmost thoughts, songs for my joy,
> utterances for my hidden griefs, and pleadings for my
> shame and my feebleness? In short whatever *finds* me,
> bears witness for itself that it has proceeded from a
> Holy Spirit, ... Why should I not believe the
> Scriptures throughout dictated, in word and thought,
> by an infallible Intelligence?". . . . Because the
> Doctrine in question petrifies at once the whole body of
> Holy Writ with all its harmonies and symmetrical
> gradations, – the flexile and the rigid, – the supporting
> hard and the clothing soft, – the blood *which is the life*, –
> the intelligencing nerves, and the rudely woven, but
> soft and springy, cellular substance, in which all are
> imbedded and lightly bound together. . . . Because the
> Doctrine evacuates of all sense and efficacy the sure and
> constant tradition, that all the several books bound up

together in our precious family Bible were composed in
different and widely distant ages, under the greatest
diversity of circumstances, and degrees of light and
information, and yet that the composers, whether as
uttering or as recording what was uttered and what was
done, were all actuated by a pure and holy Spirit, one
and the same – (for is there any spirit pure and holy, and
yet not proceeding from God – and yet not proceeding
in and with the Holy Spirit?) – one Spirit, working
diversly, now awakening strength, and now glorifying
itself in weakness, now giving power and direction to
knowledge, and now taking away the sting from error!

S.T. Coleridge, *Confessions of an Inquiring Spirit*
(1840), pp.294; 305-306.

The philosophical nature of Coleridge's response to the
threat that Roman Catholic Emancipation appeared to offer to
the Church of England ensured it an influence beyond that of
any merely political pronouncement.

The *Christian* Church, as such, has no *nationality*
entrusted to its charge. It forms no counter-balance to
the collective *heritage* of the realm. The phrase, Church
and State, has a sense and a propriety in reference to the
National Church alone. The Church of Christ cannot
be placed in this conjunction and antithesis without
forfeiting the very name of Christian. The true and only
contra-position of the Christian Church is to the world.
Her paramount aim and object, indeed, is *another*
world, not a world *to come* exclusively, but likewise
another world that now is, and to the concerns of which
alone the epithet spiritual, can without a mischievous
abuse of the word be applied.

S.T. Coleridge, *On the Constitution of Church and
State* (1830), p.117.

The full implication of the distinction Coleridge made between
the idea of a National Church as a third estate of the realm, the
Church of England in particular and the Universal Christian

Church, was rarely perceived by his followers but Thomas and
Matthew Arnold took from it the sense of a National Church
as guardian of the nation's cultural welfare, whilst Maurice and
the Christian Socialists concentrated on the realisation of the
Church of Christ on earth.

Thomas Arnold and Moral Leadership

The vision of moral leadership to be provided by a united
church which is expounded in *The Principles of Church
Reform* (1833) receives concise expression in a preface to a
volume of sermons. To preserve England from the threatened
dissolution of the tie linking Church and State, Arnold argues
for a broad church capable of incorporating the majority of
Christian worshippers. This is to be achieved by minimising
dogma and increasing the part played by the laity in
disciplinary matters. Arnold's proposals were founded upon a
sense of the radical Christian remedies demanded in response
to the nation's desperate plight.

> Great as is the falsehood of Mr. Newman's system, it
> would be but an unsatisfactory work to clear it away, if
> we had no positive truth to offer in its room. But the
> thousands of good men whom it has beguiled, because
> it professed to meet the earnest craving of their minds
> for a restoration of Christ's church with power, need
> not fear to open their eyes to its hollowness; like the
> false miracles of fraud or sorcery, it is but the
> counterfeit of a real truth. The restoration of the
> church, is, indeed, the best consummation of all our
> prayers and all our labours; it is not a dream, not a
> prospect to be seen only in the remotest distance; it is
> possible, it lies very near us; with God's blessing it is in
> the power of this very generation to begin and make
> some progress in the work. If the many good, and wise,
> and influential laymen of our Church would but awake
> to their true position and duties, and would labour
> heartily to procure for the church a living organization
> and an effective government, in both of which the laity

should be essential members, then indeed the church would become a reality. This is not Erastianism, or rather, it is not what is commonly cried down under that name; it is not the subjection of the church to the state, which, indeed, would be a most miserable and most unchristian condition; but it would be the deliverance of the church, and its exaltation to its own proper sovereignty. . . .

When we look at the condition of our country; at the poverty and wretchedness of so large a portion of the working classes; at the intellectual and moral evils which certainly exist among the poor, but by no means amongst the poor only; and when we witness the many partial attempts to remedy those evils, – attempts benevolent indeed and wise, so far as they go, but utterly unable to strike to the heart of the mischief; can any Christian doubt that here is the work for the church of Christ to do; that none else can do it; and that with the blessing of her Almighty Head she can? Looking upon the chaos around us, one power alone can reduce it into order, and fill it with light and life. And does he really apprehend the perfections and high calling of Christ's church, does he indeed fathom the depths of man's wants, or has he learnt to rise to the fulness of the stature of their divine remedy, who comes forward to preach to us the necessity of apostolic succession?

Thomas Arnold, *Christian Life, its course, its hindrances and its helps*, ed. Mrs W.E. Forster (1878), Vol. IV, pp.xlviii-li.

In one sense the catalogue of Arnold's sermon titles (e.g. 'The Necessity of Christian Exertion', 'I put away childish things', 'Moral thoughtfulness') could give a convincing portrait of the intensity of moral feeling fuelling his teaching. His pupils at Rugby, future Broad Churchmen and doubters alike, paid tribute to his towering capacity for moral leadership and in this light his son Matthew's view of religion as 'morality touched with emotion' is scarcely surprising. Higher criticism proved little threat to a man who saw it as a mere extension of the

classical scholarship in which he daily engaged. For Arnold at
the heart of Scripture lay, not a revelation of dogma, but a
moral guide to the practice of Christian life.

> But when we talk of understanding the Bible, so as to be
> guided by it amidst the infinite varieties of opinion and
> practice which beset us on every side, it is the wildest
> folly to talk of it as being, in this sense, its own
> interpreter. Our comfort is, not that it can be
> understood without study, but with it; that the same
> pains which enable us to understand heathen writings,
> whose meaning is of infinitely less value to us, will
> enable us, with God's blessing, to understand the
> Scriptures also. Neither do I mean, that mere
> intellectual study would make them clear to the careless
> or the undevout; but, supposing us to seek honestly to
> know God's will, and to pray devoutly for His help to
> guide us to it, then our study is not vain nor uncertain;
> the mind of the Scriptures may be discovered; we may
> distinguish plainly between what is clear and what is
> not clear; and what is not clear will be found far less in
> amount, and infinitely less in importance, than what is
> clear. . . .
> It is not, therefore, without great and reasonable
> hope, that we may devote ourselves to the study of the
> Scriptures; and those habits of study which are
> cultivated here, and in other places of the same kind, are
> the best ordinary means of arriving at the truth. We are
> constantly engaged in extracting the meaning of those
> who have written in times past, and in a dead language.
> We do this according to certain rules, acknowledged as
> universally as the laws of physical science: these rules
> are developed gradually, – from the simple grammar
> which forms our earliest lessons, to the rules of higher
> criticism, still no less acknowledged, which are
> understood by those of a more advanced age. And we
> do this for heathen writings; but the process is exactly
> the same – and we continually apply it, also, for that
> very purpose – with what is required to interpret the
> Word of God. After all is done, we shall still, no doubt,

find that the Scripture has its parables, its passages which cannot now be understood; but we shall find, also, that by much the larger portion of it may be clearly and certainly known; enough to be, in all points which really concern our faith and practice, a lantern to our feet, and an enlightener to our souls.

Ibid, pp.286-88.

The appearance of Thomas Hughes's novel, *Tom Brown's Schooldays* (1857), and a review which Matthew Arnold felt portrayed his father as 'a narrow bustling fanatic' seem to have prompted the elegiac tribute 'Rugby Chapel' fifteen years after his father's death.

As a whole 'Rugby Chapel' presents a fascinating synthesis of Matthew's concerns and favourite imagery. His lifelong feeling of never having been able to prove himself to his father, touched on indirectly elsewhere in his poetry, does not, even here, surface as an egocentric concern. Instead, in expressing private loss in public typology, Matthew is able to relate a personal sense of a diminished life whose goal is disconcertingly shapeless: 'to strive / Not without action to die / Fruitless, but something to snatch from dull oblivion' to a more generally pervasive sense of living in an age where meaninglessness and isolation threaten.

His father becomes one of the last examples of a heroism no longer possible. This in turn gives a value and meaning to the endeavours of the past which enables Matthew to cling to a notion of immortality, however unorthodox.

> But thou would'st not *alone*
> Be saved, my father! *alone*
> Conquer and come to thy goal,
> Leaving the rest in the wild.
> We were weary, and we
> Fearful, and we in our march
> Fain to drop down and to die,
> Still thou turnedst, and still
> Beckonedst the trembler, and still
> Gavest the weary thy hand.

If, in the paths of the world,
Stones might have wounded thy feet.
Toil or dejection have tried
Thy spirit, of that we saw
Nothing – to us thou wast still
Cheerful, and helpful, and firm!
Therefore to thee it was given
Many to save with thyself;
And, at the end of thy day,
O faithful shepherd! to come,
Bringing thy sheep in thy hand.

And through thee I believe
In the noble and great who are gone;
Pure souls honoured and blest
By former ages, who else –
Such, so soulless, so poor,
Is the race of men whom I see –
Seemed but a dream of the heart,
Seemed but a cry of desire.
Yes! I believe that there lived
Others like thee in the past,
Not like the men of the crowd
Who all round me to-day
Bluster or cringe, and make life
Hideous, and arid, and vile;
But souls tempered with fire,
Fervent, heroic, and good,
Helpers and friends of mankind.

Servants of God! – or sons
Shall I not call you? because
Not as servants ye knew
Your Father's innermost mind,
His, who unwillingly sees
One of his little ones lost –
Yours is the praise, if mankind
Hath not as yet in its march
Fainted, and fallen, and died!

M. Arnold, 'Rugby Chapel' (1860), ll.124–70.

It is worth noting in this excerpt the ambiguity of imagery which allows Dr Arnold a Christ-like status as God's faithful shepherd and son. Dr Arnold is saved in this poem from mere heroic brawn by the implication of misery and doubts suppressed – a facet which found a secular equivalent in the son's decision to abandon poetry as not morally useful.

Christian Socialism

Frederick Denison Maurice was not a Broad Churchman in Arnold's sense of comparative indifference to dogma. Rather, as the passage below indicates, he was to formulate the theological basis to Christian Socialism. For him the Universal Church is a living part of the divine kingdom, thriving upon and stimulating the unity of men in Christ. Maurice, a man of Unitarian background, believed that the Church of England was best equipped to fulfil this function. Christ provides a living ground of unity because the Incarnation was not a once-and-for-all revelation but continues within each human soul. Therefore, he argues, the Christian message should not start with the Fall and original sin but with our creation as fellow members of Christ.

> The idea of the Church, as a united body, has been put forth, chiefly to shew the wickedness of those who have separated from it. Its episcopacy and its sacraments have been looked upon chiefly as exclusive of those who have them not. Above all, the spiritual character of the Church as deriving its life from its head, a character which the Dissenters are especially disposed by their profession to recognise, has been disjoined from the institutions which embody it. Men have been asked to receive these institutions which embody it. Men have been asked to receive these institutions merely as such, and then to hope for spiritual life through them. Little attempt has been made to prove to them that the institutions are themselves living portions of the divine kingdom. A person therefore who has entered into these convictions himself, will not despair of seeing all

the true hearty Dissenters gradually receiving them also. . . .

Or does the Churchman I am supposing find himself in one of our awful manufacturing districts? Of course, the sense of his own utter inadequacy to deal with the mass of evil which he meets there is the first which will take hold of him, and will grow stronger every day. . . . More impressive by far was the speech of the Methodist and the Evangelical: 'You have immortal souls, they are perishing; oh! ask how they may be saved.' Such words spoken with true earnestness are very mighty. But they are not enough; men feel that they are not merely lost creatures; they look up to heaven above them, and ask whether it can be true that this is the whole account of their condition; that their sense of right and wrong, their cravings for fellowship, their consciousness of being creatures having powers which no other creatures possess, are all nothing. If religion, they say, will give us no explanation of these feelings, if it can only tell us about a fall for the whole race, and an escape for a few individuals of it, then our wants must be satisfied without religion. Then begin Chartism and Socialism, and whatever schemes make rich men tremble. Surely, what the modern assertors of a Church system say about the duty of administering active charity to these sufferers, of shewing that we do not merely regard them as pensioners on the national bounty, but as fellow-men for whom we are to make sacrifices – surely this language is far more to the purpose. Surely if acted upon even imperfectly, it must produce most happy effects. But how would the proclamation to our Chartists and Socialists, that they had baptismal purity once, and that they have lost it now; that they must recover their ground by repentance, by prayer and fasting; that they must submit to discipline, and be deprived of privileges which they never exercised nor cared for; how can such a proclamation as this meet any of the confused, disorderly notions which are stirring in their minds, or set them right?

On the other hand, if the new and unwonted

proclamation were to go forth, 'God has cared for you, you are indeed his children; his Son has redeemed you, his Spirit is striving with you; there is a fellowship larger, more irrespective of outward distinctions, more democratical, than any which you can create; but it is a fellowship of mutual love, not mutual selfishness, in which the chief of all is the servant of all – may not one think that a result would follow as great as that which attended the preaching of any Franciscan friar in the twelfth century, or any Methodist preacher in the eighteenth? For these are true words, everlasting words and yet words which belong especially to our time; they are words which interpret and must be interpreted by that regular charity, that ministerial holiness, those sacraments, prayers and discipline, of which the Catholic speaks. They connect his words about repentance with those of the Evangelical, making it manifest, that nothing but an accursed nature and a depraved will could have robbed any of the blessings which God has bestowed upon us all. They translate into meaning and life all the liberal plans for the education of adults and children; they enable us to fulfil the notion, which statesmen have entertained, that the Church is to be the supporter of the existing orders, by making her a teacher and example to those orders respecting their duties and responsibilities; by removing the hatred which their forgetfulness of those duties and responsibilities is threatening to create in the minds of the lower classes.

F.D. Maurice, *The Kingdom of Christ* (1883),
Vol. II, pp.416-20.

This emphasis on communion in Christ led to Maurice's involvement in the Christian Socialist movement, which saw itself as involved in conflict with 'unsocial Christians and the unchristian socialists'. In the year when Chartist threats of violence had followed in the wake of the 1848 European revolutions, Maurice, a barrister named Ludlow and Charles Kingsley banded together to convince the workers of their need for a Christian basis to social change. Prepared to listen to and talk with atheistic socialists, to contribute practical endeavour in setting up working men's cooperative associations, they gradually gained Chartist recognition. The movement as such petered out in 1855 and Maurice turned his attention to working men's education.

Maurice's inclusion under the label 'Broad Church' stems from the sympathetic friendship he extended to the unorthodox and the doubters and from his teaching which denied eternal punishment to be compatible with a loving God. This combination of factors was largely responsible for his dismissal from the Professorship of Divinity at King's College, London.

Christian Socialism produced two famous literary apologists: Charles Kingsley and Thomas Hughes. *Yeast* (1848) and *Alton Locke* (1850) demonstrate Kingsley's social and moral concern particularly clearly. (Incidentally Chapter 36 of *Alton Locke* also makes it clear that Kingsley found it possible to reconcile evolutionary theory with his religious faith.) Kingsley's novels (see pp.37–38), like Hughes's, display a distinctly pugnacious character. In both men fighting for the right and defending the underprivileged appeared to bring with them the irresistible challenge of humiliating the bully, whether he appeared in the establishment garb of aristocrat, as priest, as the profiteer of sweatshops or as the school tyrant. In Kingsley's case literary fisticuffs were sometimes a means of keeping doubt at bay. Thomas Hughes's 'muscular Christianity', as this school of religious conduct became known, was of a yet simpler kind. *Tom Brown's Schooldays* (1857) was intended as a tribute to the educational example provided by Dr Arnold's Rugby, where Hughes had been a pupil. In Hughes's novel, however, the inward moral seriousness found in Dr Arnold and his closest pupils is transformed into the ethics of the team spirit and 'manly virtues', whilst these men's anti-dogmatism is misinterpreted as anti-intellectualism. As the popular hero, head of eleven, puts it in the course of a moral pep-talk, designed to defend the Doctor's reforming ways, 'I know I'd sooner win two school-house matches running than get the Balliol scholarship any day – (frantic cheers)' (Ch. 6). Canvassing his own interests

Hughes also includes a vignette of the ideal Christian Socialist parson who goes to work in 'a very nest of Chartism and Atheism' and wins the respect of masters and men, Christians and freethinkers alike (Part I, Ch. 2.).

Benjamin Jowett and *Essays and Reviews*

Benjamin Jowett, Regius Professor of Greek at Oxford, was one of a group of seven liberal churchmen (Pattison was another) (see pp.41–42) who in 1860 published *Essays and Reviews*. Their aim was to promote free discussion of contemporary critical ideas concerning the Bible. By training a classical scholar, Jowett was anxious to promote the critical examination of the Biblical text in the manner employed to interpret other classical texts: that is, to set each portion of the Bible in its historical context and endeavour to discover the 'one meaning' which it had in the mind of its initial author and audience. By divesting Scripture of its dogmatic accretions, Jowett maintained, the Victorian obsession with the conflict between reason and faith could be dissipated. Jowett was not a Rationalist. He wanted men also to be able to perceive the spirit of the Bible, to feel the presence of God and the mind of Christ in Scripture and to recognise the ethical teaching revealed in the life of Christ. At the top of the catalogue of virtues enshrined in the Gospel, Broad Churchmen placed truth. The spirit of the essayists' enterprise is captured in Jowett's concluding paragraphs.

> The Scripture nowhere leads us to suppose that the circumstance of all men speaking well of us is any ground for supposing that we are acceptable in the sight of God. And there is no reason why the condemnation of others should be witnessed to by our own conscience. . . . He who takes the prevailing opinions of Christians and decks them out in their gayest colours – who reflects the better mind of the world to itself – is likely to be its favourite teacher. In that ministry of the Gospel, even when assuming forms repulsive to persons of education, no doubt the good is far greater

than the error or harm. But there is also a deeper work which is not dependent on the opinions of men in which many elements combine, some alien to religion, or accidentally at variance with it. That work can hardly expect to win much popular favour, so far as it runs counter to the feelings of religious parties. But he who bears a part in it may feel a confidence, which no popular caresses or religious sympathy could inspire, that he has by a Divine help been enabled to plant his foot somewhere beyond the waves of time. He may depart hence before the natural term, worn out with intellectual toil; regarded with suspicion by many of his contemporaries; yet not without a sure hope that the love of truth, which men of saintly lives often seem to slight, is, nevertheless, accepted before God.

B. Jowett, 'On the Inspiration of Scripture' (1860),
Essays and Reviews, pp.432-33.

The following extract parodying a sermon by Jowett comes from a *roman à clef*, *The New Republic*, by William Hurrell Mallock. Nephew to Hurrell and J.A. Froude and himself an Anglo-Catholic, Mallock's intense dislike of the Liberal theology of the Broad Church was fostered by spending his undergraduate days at Balliol, where Jowett was Master. The novel first appeared anonymously in magazine form. In a recast version, the novel of 1877 bore the subtitle 'Culture, Faith and Philosophy in an English Country House'. Leading intellectual figures of the day, including Arnold, Pater, Ruskin, Pusey, Jowett, W.K. Clifford, Tyndall and Huxley, walk the pages of this satirical novel.

The benignly vacuous style of Mallock's preacher comes uncomfortably close to pastiche as Mallock captures Jowett's blend of spiritual devotion and anti-dogmatism. Nevertheless the concluding sentences leave us in no doubt as to Mallock's essential objection to the reductionism implicit in these 'eternal vagaries'.

'*Thus we see,*' said the Doctor cheerfully, looking around him with a smile of benignant triumph, and blinking with his eyes, 'that difference of opinion about the dogmas of religion is nothing new. It existed in the Jewish Church, the phenomenon was only prolonged by Christianity. Later Judaism and primitive Christianity were both made up of a variety of systems, all honestly and boldly thought out, differing widely from each other, and called by the honourable appellation of heresies: and of these, let me remind you, it is the glory of the Church of England to be composed likewise.

'Nor is this all,' he went on in a softer and more appealing tone; 'not only are all these things so confused and doubtful; but we now see that, in the face of recent criticism, we cannot even be quite sure about any of the details of the divine life of our Lord. But in all this' – the Doctor's voice here became still more aërial, and he fixed his eyes upon the painted ceiling of the theatre, as though he were gazing on some glorious vision – 'in all this there is nothing to discompose us. We can be quite sure that He lived, and that He went about doing good, and that in him we have, in the highest sense, everlasting life.

'Let us then no longer fight against the conclusions of science and of criticism, but rather see in them the hand of God driving us, even against our will, away from beliefs and teachings that are not really those of His son. If we do not do this – if we persist in identifying the false Christianity with the true – the false, when it is at last plucked rudely away from us, as it must be, will carry away a part of the true with it. And as long as we are in this state of mind, we are never for a moment safe. We can never open a philological review, or hear of a scientific experiment, without trembling. Witness the discussions now engaging so much public attention on the subject of animal automatism, and the marvellous results which experiments on living subjects have of late days revealed to us; a frog with half a brain having destroyed more theology than all the doctors of the Church with their whole brains can ever build up again. Thus does God choose the "weak things of this world to confound the wise." Seeing, then, that this is the state of

> the case, we should surely learn henceforth not to
> identify Christianity with anything that science can
> assail, or even question. Let us say rather that nothing is
> or can be essential to the religion of Christ which, when
> once stated, can be denied without absurdity. If we can
> only attain to this conception, we shall see truly that this
> our faith is indeed one "that no man taketh away from
> us.'

> W.H. Mallock, *The New Republic* (1877), Book 2,
> Ch. 1.

Arthur Penrhyn Stanley and the Church United in the Pursuit of Truth

Thomas Arnold's pupil and biographer, Stanley, had refused to contribute to *Essays and Reviews*. However once the storm of protest broke, Stanley defended the *septem contra Christum*, as they were popularly known. Whilst deploring the negative tone apparent in some of the contributions, Stanley was anxious to defend the essayists' right to hold these views within the Established Church. The assembled bishops had questioned the compatibility of such lax views on inspiration with the continued subscription to the *Thirty Nine Articles* on the part of the six clerical essayists. Subsequent legal proceedings against two of the essayists resulted in their eventually (1864) being cleared of heresy. Newman's question about the nature of the Church's authority and its relation to the state (see pp.25–27) had been posed in acute form in this case. Stanley's efforts were directed to ensuring that the state guaranteed the right of the Church's clergy to pursue the truth. Aware that the essayists trod 'on difficult and shifting ground', Stanley feared that 'the kernel of truth' they nobly sought might be sacrificed for the shell of orthodoxy.

> The style, the manner, the composition of this book
> may be offensive or peculiar. But facts and creeds are
> not revolutionised by manner and style. The principles,

1. George Eliot in 1865. A drawing in chalks by Sir Frederick Burton.

2. Frontispiece to J. Purchas *The Directorium Anglicanum* (1858). See pages 43-44.

3. *Christ in the House of his Parents*. Painting by John Everett Millais, 1849-50. The composition observes the Oxford Movement's sacramental view of church architecture.

4. *Family Prayers*. Painting by Samuel Butler, 1864.

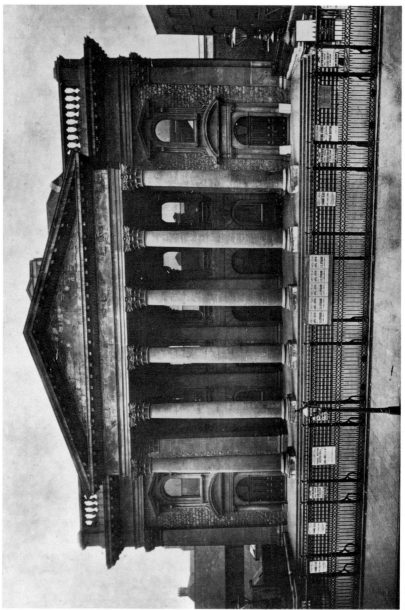

5. The Metropolitan Tabernacle. See page 89.

even the words, of the Essayists have been known for
the last fifty years, through writings popular amongst
all English students of the higher branches of theology.
If there be a conspiracy, it is one far more formidable
than that of the seven Essayists. For it is a conspiracy in
which half the rising generation, one quarter of the
Bench of Bishops, the most leading spirits of our clergy,
have been, and are, and will be engaged, whatever be the
results of the present controversy. Coleridge led the
way. A whole generation arose under his Germanising
influence. Even Dr. Pusey swelled the ranks for a time,
and still retains in his teaching traces of his former
associates. . . . Arnold's 'Life and Letters' has been
allowed to pass through as many editions as the 'Essays
and Reviews,' and yet contains not only all the
fundamental principles of the present volume, which
have been so much attacked, but particular passages
almost verbally coincident with the language of
Professor Jowett or Dr. Williams on the 'Book of
Daniel,' or even of Mr. Wilson on the early Jewish
history. . . .
This common challenge is unquestionably the one
common ground between the seven authors. Every one
of them by lending his name to the book does beyond
doubt assert that, however much he may differ from the
views contained in any other essay than his own, he yet
vindicates the lawfulness of holding those views within
the English Church. . . . The lay contributor, however
offensive his statements, is dismissed 'as comparatively
blameless.' But the Christian minister, it is said, has
'parted with his natural liberty.' It is almost openly
avowed (and we are sorry to see this tendency as much
amongst free-thinking laymen as amongst fanatical
clergymen) that Truth was made for the laity and
Falsehood for the clergy – that Truth is tolerable
everywhere except in the mouths of the ministers of the
God of Truth – that Falsehood, driven from every other
quarter of the educated world, may find an honoured
refuge behind the consecrated bulwarks of the
Sanctuary.

Against this godless theory of a national Church we solemnly protest. It is a theory tainted with a far deeper unbelief than any that has ever been charged against the Essayists and Reviewers.

A.P. Stanley, 'Judgement on *Essays and Reviews*', *Edinburgh Review*, Vol. 130 (1861), pp.480-81; 489-90.

It is the collective message of Stanley's hymns that strikes the reader rather than individual felicities of expression. His eclecticism and anti-dogmatic stand are seen in the recurrence of two related themes: God's revelation is not limited to specific events of Christian narrative but occurs whenever the truth triumphs. For this reason the Church must look for unity on a broad base.

The Lord is come! Dull hearts to wake,
He speaks, as never man yet spake,
The Truth which makes His servants free,
The Royal Law of Liberty.
Though heav'n and earth shall pass away,
His living words our spirits stay,
And from His treasures, new and old,
Th' eternal mysteries unfold.

The Lord is come! In ev'ry heart,
Where Truth and Mercy claim a part;
In every land where Right is Might,
And deeds of darkness shun the light;
In every church, where Faith and Love
Lift earthward thoughts to things above;
In every holy, happy home,
We bless Thee, Lord, that Thou hast come!

*   *   *

When diverging creeds shall learn
Towards their central Source to turn;
When contending churches tire
Of the earthquake, wind, and fire;
Here let strife and clamour cease
At that still, small voice of peace –
'May they all united be
In the Father and in Me.'

*　　*　　*

Christ is risen! The Truth that died
Mock'd and scourged and crucified,
Still unquestion'd mounts on high
Next to God's own Majesty.

Christ is risen! Deep within
Every charnel-house of sin
Lives a spark which yet may shine
Radiant with the life divine.

> 'Hymn for Advent', vv.2 and 6; 'This do in
> remembrance of me' v.5; and 'Easter', vv.4 and 5,
> *Letters and Verses of A.P. Stanley*, ed. R.E. Prothero
> (1895), pp.370-71; 404; 406.

Stanley's determined concentration on areas of ethical consensus produces verse in which abstract nouns and the monochromatic imagery conveying a universe where the light of Truth will finally overcome the gloom of sin and error predominate. Stanley's headnote to the Eucharistic hymn describes it as 'a Sacramental Hymn founded on the one common idea of a commemoration which lies at the basis of all views of the Eucharist', thus dismissing the profound theological disagreement which existed as to the nature of the Sacrament. Such well-intentioned evasiveness goes far to explaining the Evangelical Shaftesbury's diary entry on the day of Stanley's induction as Dean of Westminster Abbey. 'So Stanley entered on his infidel and mischievous career in Westminster, corrupting the clergy, corrupting society by the

balmy poison of his doctrine. ... Misleading, lulling,
entrapping weak souls, and betraying in every word of his
mouth, and every stroke of his pen, "the Son of Man with a
kiss"!'

Two Laymen Respond to Broad Church Teaching

Few poems give better indication than *In Memoriam* of the
thin line which separated the liberal speculation of Broad
Churchmen from the realms of honest doubt. The two sections
reprinted in this book (see pp.107–108) were immediately
juxtaposed by Tennyson. In this monumental elegy Tennyson
raises many of the problems that beset would-be believers of
his day. If man could be seen as merely another passing
phenomenon of a materialist universe, then the defence of a
spiritual view of man seemed to rest increasingly heavily on
notions of the soul's immortality. But might not man have
been led to picture a comforting after-life precisely as a way of
promising significance to a life which seemed so bedevilled by
random destruction? In such moods Tennyson's reading of
Lyell (see pp.105–107) seemed to make it certain that man could
no longer see nature as the revelation of God's handiwork.
Faith and hope, as Broad Churchmen like Jowett freely
admitted, must then be redefined as a matter of inner
conviction and the will to believe.

> The wish, that of the living whole
>   No life may fail beyond the grave,
>   Derives it not from what we have
> The likest God within the soul?
>
> Are God and Nature then at strife,
>   That Nature lends such evil dreams?
>   So careful of the type she seems,
> So careless of the single life;
>
> That I, considering everywhere
>   Her secret meaning in her deeds,
>   And finding that of fifty seeds
> She often brings but one to bear,

I falter where I firmly trod,
And falling with my weight of cares
Upon the great world's altar-stairs
That slope through darkness up to God,

I stretch lame hands of faith, and grope,
And gather dust and chaff, and call
To what I feel is Lord of all,
And faintly trust the larger hope.

Lord Tennyson, *In Memoriam* (1850), LV. (This
section written 'some years before' 1844.)

Tennyson's verse conveys the sense of the ground failing
beneath his feet as one world picture dissolves. The ABBA
stanza form of the entire poem which so effectively mirrors the
wavering graph of Tennyson's emotions and the circling
processes of thought which found logic inadequate here convey·
the polarities between which the poem oscillates as those two
final stanzas swing between 'I' and 'God', 'I' and 'hope'.
Between self and other all is uncertain as each positive or
known quantity (e.g. 'firmly', 'stretch', 'hands') is undermined
by a negative (e.g. 'fall', 'grope', 'lame').

Trollope's thumbnail sketch of the new brand of clergy of
liberal persuasion indicates the thinking but puzzled layman's
response to Broad Church theology. He is referring to the case
which had arisen when the Bishop of Natal, Colenso, had
published a book on the Pentateuch in which he essayed to
prove that these Biblical writings were the product of a variety
of sources and that furthermore they could not everywhere be
accorded the status of historical record. Attempts to depose
Colenso as heretical encountered a series of legal obstacles
which involved the rights of the Established Church in
England to legislate in the affairs of the Anglican Church
abroad when Church and State were independent of one
another. Uninterested in the precise legal or theological
niceties of this particular case, Trollope lists the catch-phrases
which symbolise a whole body of Broad Church teaching. His
own nostalgia for the certainty offered by the old orthodoxy
and his knowledge that such innocence is now irretrievable is a

conservative version of the painful loss experienced by Clough or Arnold. Rather than reserving his fire for a new generation of leaders who disappoint orthodox expectations, Trollope imaginatively extends his sympathies to encompass the spiritual travails of such men. Nor does he fail to remind his readers of the social and moral opprobrium such clergy face.

We can only observe our new rector, and find out from his words and his acts how his own mind works on these subjects.

It is soon manifest to us that he has accepted the teaching of the rocks and stones, and that we may give up the actual six days, and give up also the deluge as a drowning of all the world. Indeed, we had almost come to fancy that even the old rector had become hazy on these points. And gradually there leak out to us, as to the falling of manna from heaven, and as to the position of Jonah within the whale, and as to the speaking of Balaam's ass, certain doubts, not expressed indeed, but which are made manifest to us as existing by the absence of expressions of belief. In the intercourse of social life we see something of a smile cross our new friend's face when the thirty-nine articles are brought down beneath his nose. Then he has read the *Essays and Reviews*, and will not declare his opinion that the writers of them should be unfrocked and sent away into chaos; – nay, we find that he is on terms of personal intimacy with one at least among the number of those writers. And, lastly, there comes out a subscription list for Bishop Colenso, and we find our new rector's name down for a five-pound note! That we regard as the sign, to be recognized by us as the most certain of all signs, that he has cut the rope which bound his barque to the old shore, and that he is going out to sea in quest of a better land. Shall we go with him, or shall we stay where we are?

If one could stay, if one could only have a choice in the matter, if one could really believe that the old shore is best, who would leave it? Who would not wish to be secure if he knew where security lay? But this new teacher, who has come among us with his ill-defined doctrines and his subrisive smile, – he and they who have taught him, – have made it impossible for us to stay. With hands outstretched towards the old places, with sorrowing hearts, – with hearts which still love the old teachings which the mind will no longer accept, – we, too, cut our ropes, and go out in our little boats, and search for a land that will be new to us, though how far new, – new in how many things, we do not know. Who would not stay behind if it were possible to him?

But our business at present is with the teacher, and not with the taught. Of him we may declare that he is, almost always, a true man, – true in spite of that subrisive smile and ill-defined doctrine. He is one who without believing, cannot bring himself to think that he believes, or to say that he believes that which he disbelieves without grievous suffering to himself. He has to say it, and does suffer. ... He had, by the subscription, attached himself to the Broad Church with the newest broad principles, and must expect henceforth to be regarded as little better than an infidel, – certainly as an enemy in the camp, – by the majority of his brethren of the day. "Why does he not give up his tithes? Why does he stick to his temporalities?" says the old-fashioned, wrathful parson of the neighbouring parish; and the sneer, which is repeated from day to day and from month to month, is not slow to reach the new man's ear. It is an accusation hard to be borne; but it has to be borne, – among other things, – by the clergyman who subscribes for Colenso.

A. Trollope, 'The Clergyman who subscribes for Colenso', *Clergymen of the Church of England* (1866), pp.127-30.

4 Dissent

Many works on nineteenth-century religious thought shy away from the Dissenting world as being both peripheral to the intellectual life of the period and too diverse for brief justice to be done. I have not attempted to represent the doctrinal variations to be found within Nonconformity, which at the most extreme range from Unitarianism, thin on dogma and strong beyond its numbers in the Victorian intellectual milieu and the circles of social reform, to the dogmatic precision of rigorously exclusive sects like the Strict Baptists. Inevitably the various limbs of this doctrinally heterogenous body came to terms with Biblical criticism and evolutionary theory at substantially differing rates. Early in the nineteenth century, however, the division between the old style Dissenters such as Presbyterians, Baptists, Independents or Quakers and the new sects thrown up by the mid-eighteenth century Evangelical Revival became less marked as the Evangelical spirit became more broadly diffused and High Calvinism more rarely affirmed.

For those writing about Dissent the variety of possible doctrines or practices made it possible to pillory it as either the religion of the uneducated and violently emotional *or* the parochial expression of the complacent philistinism associated with classes in trade. Nonconformity might also be presented as so well-established as to lack all capacity for Protestant dissent or as the natural home for the dissatisfied or the spiritually footloose.

The extracts in this chapter were not chosen with an eye to justice of numerical representation but rather to indicate typical Dissenting concerns of the period. The first portion of the chapter attempts to convey something of the changing face, or faces, of Dissent whilst the second half concentrates more upon the quality of Dissenting life and worship. Politically speaking Nonconformity was a recognisable force in the Victorian period, although its bite was often less effective than its bark, partly because different sects and leaders assessed the political and religious priorities differently. The Nonconformist conscience, as it became known towards the end of the century, was seen at work politically and socially, devoting particular care to the politically disadvantaged and the socially outcast and deprived.

At the local level the life of the chapel could form the centre of a member's social experience, offering an attractive, though often no less hierarchically structured, alternative community to those found through daily work. Although Nonconformists varied, as in all else, in the importance they attached to church order and a formal liturgy, they were agreed on the importance of the Word. The internal architecture of many a conventicle reflected the focal role of the preacher whose practised eloquence indeed occasionally became the immediate motive for erecting a more commodious 'preaching house'.

Dissenting interest in the Word might lead one to expect a flourishing literary tradition, to look for the natural successors of Bunyan, Isaac Watts or the Wesley brothers. It is possible to point to the novels of the Unitarian Elizabeth Gaskell or to the Dissenting tradition in which Robert Browning grew up, yet, on the whole, the nineteenth century does not emerge as a strong period in Dissenting literary culture. This was not just a matter of opposition to fiction or distrust of the imagination but rather reflected the preoccupations of Dissenting leaders of the period. Disadvantaged politically and educationally at the beginning of the century, Dissenters expended much energy on removing these disabilities and upon activities more easily discernible as theocentric, such as philanthropic work, than literary endeavour seemed to be.

Nevertheless sermons and hymns proliferated and it is possible to find generous portraits of Dissenters in such novels as Elizabeth Gaskell's *Ruth* or *Cousin Phillis* or George Eliot's *Adam Bede* or *Felix Holt*.

The Changing Faces of Dissent

Sectarianism and the 'Pursuit of Purity'

Newman allowed his satirical impulse free rein in his novel *Loss and Gain* when he came to depict the volatile nature of the new Dissent of the 1830s. On the eve of his secession to Rome Charles Reding, the novel's hero, is visited by a series of representatives of recently formed sects. The various seceders from Anglicanism share the pursuit of renewing the apostolic purity of the Early Church and a conviction of the scriptural authority underlying their newly formulated doctrines. Together they form a tableau illustrating Newman's thesis that religious systems lacking the authority offered in the traditional development of dogma must necessarily founder upon the competing assertions of private judgement.

The curious combination of kitchen boy and gentleman that first appears contains Newman's comment on the need to impose a hierarchical structure of authority, however ludicrous, on the oddly assorted congregation who had flocked to the Rev. Edward Irving and then discarded him when he was discovered not to possess the 'gift of tongues' his preaching had done so much to encourage.

> '[I] am a member of the Holy Catholic Church, assembling in Huggermugger Lane. "Ah," said Charles, "I see; that's what the 'gods' call you; now, what do men?" "Men," said Jack, not understanding, however, the allusion – "men call us Christians, professing the opinions of the late Rev. Edward Irving, B.D." "I understand perfectly now," said Reding; "Irvingites – I recollect" – "No, sir," he said, "not Irvingites; we do not follow man; we follow wherever the Spirit leads us; we have given up Tongue. But I ought to introduce you to my friend, who is more than an Angel," he proceeded modestly, "who has more than the tongue of men and angels, being nothing short of an Apostle, sir. Mr. Reding, here's the Rev. Alexander Highfly. Mr. Highfly, this is Mr. Reding."
> Mr. Highfly was a man of gentlemanlike appearance and manner; his language was refined, and his conduct was delicate; so much so that Charles at once changed his tone in speaking to him. . . . "It is, I recollect, one of the characteristics of your body," said Charles, "to have an order of Apostles, in addition to Bishops, Priests, and Deacons." "Rather," said his visitor, "it is

the special characteristic; for we acknowledge the orders of the Church of England. We are but completing the Church system by restoring the Apostolic College." "What I should complain of," said Charles, "were I at all inclined to listen to your claims, would be the very different views which different members of your body put forward." "You must recollect, sir," answered Mr. Highfly, "that we are under divine teaching, and that truth is but gradually communicated to the Church. We do not pledge ourselves what we shall believe to-morrow by anything we say today." "Certainly," answered Reding, "things have been said to me by your teachers which I must suppose were only private opinions, though they seemed to be more." "But I was saying," said Mr. Highfly, "that at present we are restoring the Gentile Apostolate. The Church of England has Bishops, Priests, and Deacons, but a Scriptural Church has more; it is plain it ought to have Apostles. In Scripture, Apostles had the supreme authority, and the three Anglican orders were but subordinate to them." . . .

J.H. Newman, *Loss and Gain* (1848), Part III, Ch. 7.

The second visitor's spiritual pilgrimage finds echoes in the lives of many Anglican seceders of this period, including Newman's own brother, Frank.

"[A] young lady, not without attractions of person and dress, presented herself. . . . Some dear sisters of hers were engaged in organising a new religious body, and Mr. Reding's accession, counsel, assistance, would be particularly valuable; the more so, because as yet they had not any gentleman of University-education among them. "May I ask," said Charles, "the name of the intended persuasion?" "The name," she answered, "is not fixed; indeed, this is one of the points on which we should covet the privilege of the advice of a gentleman so well qualified as Mr. Reding to assist us in our deliberations." "And your tenets, ma'am?" "Here, too," she replied, "there is much still to be done; the tenets are not fixed either, that is, they are but sketched; and we shall prize your suggestions much. Nay, you will of course have the opportunity, as you would have the right, to nominate any doctrine to which you may be especially inclined." Charles did not know how to answer to so liberal an offer. She continued: "Perhaps it is right, Mr. Reding, that I should tell you something more about myself personally. I was born in the communion of the Church of England; for a while I was a member of the New Connexion; and at present," she added, still with drooping head and languid sing-song voice, "at present, I am a Plymouth brother." It got too absurd; and Charles, who had for an instant been amused, now became full of the one thought, how to get her out of the room. . . .

Ibid.

The third visitor is a reminder of the millenialist fervour of the period which preached that Christ's second coming would be heralded by the restoration of the Jews to the Promised Land.

"You may like to know my name; it is Zerubbabel."

Vexed as Reding was, he felt that he had no right to visit the tediousness of his former visitor upon his present; so he forced himself to reply, "Zerubbabel, indeed, and is Zerubbabel your Christian name, sir, or your surname?" "It is both at once, Mr. Reding," answered Zerubbabel, "or rather, I have no Christian name, and Zerubbabel is my one Jewish designation." "You are come, then, to inquire whether I am likely to become a Jew." "Stranger things have happened," answered his visitor; "for instance, I myself was once a deacon in the Church of England." "Then you're not a Jew?" said Charles. "I am a Jew by choice," he said; "after much prayer and study of Scripture, I have come to the conclusion, that, as Judaism was the first religion, so it's to be the last. Christianity I consider an episode in the history of revelation." "You are not likely to have many followers in such a belief," said Charles; "we are all for progress now, not for retrograding." "I differ from you, Mr. Reding," replied Zerubbabel; "see what the Establishment is doing; it has sent a Bishop to Jerusalem."

Ibid.

Anglican involvement in the appointment of a Lutheran bishop to Jerusalem in 1841 had been one of the many factors determining Newman's own secession to Roman Catholicism.

Political Dissent

When Edward Miall took up the editorship of the *Nonconformist* in 1841 he established as its motto 'The Dissidence of Dissent and the Protestantism of the Protestant Religion'. As editor of a militant organ for church disestablishment Miall entered the arena at a low ebb of Dissenting hopes. Disestablishment had seemed within Dissenting grasp to Dissenters and Anglicans alike in the early 1830s period of Whig reform but by 1841 the Dissenters' internal divisions and the Tory backlash had effectively removed this possibility. The success of Miall's plea to Dissenting ministers is attested by the historian J.R. Vincent, who remarks of their action at a local level that they formed 'a sort of Communist hard core to the popular front' (*Pollbooks* (1967), p.18). Whilst helping to explain how Dissent of all kinds continued to be tarred with the brush of radicalism by the Establishment, the passage below also demonstrates the religious conviction which inspired Miall's campaign.

AN image carved with marvellous cunning, tricked out in solemn vestments, a part woven by human fancy, a part stolen from the chest of truth – an image, we repeat, an outside semblance, a counterfeit of life, not God-created, but made by the hands of man, empty, without heart, destitute of any well-spring of vitality – has been placed by aristocratic legislation in the throne of Christianity. The living, simple, beauteous truth, the rightful queen to whom all spiritual homage of due belongs, too sincere, too earnest, too unbending for the purposes of men in power, was long since deposed, thrust out, compelled to wander in obscurity and to witness the fealty of her voluntary adherents treated as an offence against the good order of society. Great men – kings, nobles, bishops, stand round about the image their own sagacity has fashioned, bow to it and pay it court, proclaim it the only true church of Christ, pass laws, professedly to maintain its state, and share the proceeds among themselves. All men are bid to acknowledge it, in humble thankfulness that they are permitted to hold any conversation at all with her whose throne is usurped by this creature of the state. Meanwhile, these great ones, under the sanction and on the behalf of their church, perpetrate a thousand enormities, violate every maxim of religion, degrade, insult, harass, imprison – regard nor justice nor mercy in their pursuit of pelf, until half this nation, disgusted with the imposture and ignorant of the claims and worth of heavenly truth, declare that there is no such thing, that it is all a hollow pretence, and that Christianity itself is a mere scheme of priestcraft.

Christianity! What kind of Christianity is our state church upheld to subserve? An attention to rites for the performance of which fees may be exacted – heartless formality – a blind, unreasoning, ignorant, superstitious obedience to the priesthood – payment of tithes, and easter-offerings, and church-rates – these are the great objects of our establishment. The interest taken in it by our rulers is just an interest in property. What concern can the vast majority of them be supposed to feel for the spread of religion? The whole thing is a stupendous money-scheme, carried on under false pretences – a bundle of vested rights, stamped for the greater security with the sacred name of Christianity – an affair of livings, and benefices, and baronial bishoprics to the aggregate amount of 5,000,000*l.* a year.

To shatter this image, and give the dust of it to the four winds of heaven – to re-conduct Christianity to her throne – to vindicate her rights – to restore her legitimate influence – is the sacred mission of protestant dissenting ministers. They are appointed by Providence to this great work – their principles open up to them this glorious career – they are equal to the mighty undertaking – the time is come for them to decide and to act. With earnest longings of heart, with trembling solicitude largely intermingled with hope, we wait, the country waits, to hear their determination. We entreat them by all that is good and great to come forward. Let them but say, "work shall be done," and the doom of the establishment is pronounced.

For they know not their own power. They seem scarcely to be sensible of the vast things they can accomplish. They have the hearts of millions in their keeping – they enjoy the confidence of the great body of virtuous intelligence in this country. In one year they might change the whole aspect of this momentous question. The train is laid – the match is put into their hands – let them dauntlessly apply it, and the flame of enthusiasm they will kindle will astound even themselves.

Editorial by Edward Miall, *Nonconformist*, 19 May 1841.

Images of Eighteenth and Nineteenth-Century Methodism Compared

George Eliot's reflective pastoral novel *Adam Bede* looks back to Methodism as practised at the end of the eighteenth century. One of her prime concerns as a novelist was to free readers from the habit of stereotyped reactions to their fellow men. In the following passage the chosen time span endeavours to jolt the readers out of contemporary prejudices, whilst her commentary often hints at the importance of applying this lesson to the society of her own day. Methodism had

undoubtedly become less adventurous and more overtly
respectable in the intervening years but it also suited Eliot's
ideological bent to place its most attractive phase in the past
when untutored minds saw the Christian religion as the
channel for their best impulses. As the final sentence suggests
Eliot saw very little connection between doctrinal orthodoxy
and man's most humane instincts which her reading of
Feuerbach had taught her to believe as best enshrined in one's
fellow men.

> The picture we are apt to make of Methodism in our
> imagination is not an amphitheatre of green hills, or the
> deep shade of broad-leaved sycamores, where a crowd
> of rough men and weary-hearted women drank in a
> faith which was a rudimentary culture, which linked
> their thoughts with the past, lifted their imagination
> above the sordid details of their own narrow lives, and
> suffused their souls with the sense of a pitying, loving,
> infinite Presence, sweet as summer to the houseless
> needy. It is too possible that to some of my readers
> Methodism may mean nothing more than low-pitched
> gables up dingy streets, sleek grocers, sponging
> preachers, and hypocritical jargon – elements which are
> regarded as an exhaustive analysis of Methodism in
> many fashionable quarters.
>
> That would be a pity; for I cannot pretend that Seth
> and Dinah were anything else than Methodists – not
> indeed of that modern type which reads quarterly
> reviews and attends in chapels with pillared porticoes;
> but of a very old-fashioned kind. They believed in
> present miracles, in instantaneous conversions, in
> revelations by dreams and visions; they drew lots, and
> sought for Divine guidance by opening the Bible at
> hazard; having a literal way of interpreting the
> Scriptures, which is not at all sanctioned by approved
> commentators; and it is impossible for me to represent
> their diction as correct, or their instruction as liberal.
> Still – if I have read religious history aright – faith, hope,
> and charity have not always been found in a direct ratio
> with a sensibility to the three concords; and it is

possible, thank Heaven! to have very erroneous
theories and very sublime feelings.

G. Eliot, *Adam Bede* (1858), Ch. 3.

Congregationalism 1840–1890

In 1889 the Congregationalist minister R.W. Dale (1829–95)
used the opportunity of a centenary sermon at William Jay's
(1769–1853) chapel in Bath (a chapel once attended by William
Wilberforce to the subsequent embarrassment of his High
Church sons) to review the changes in Dissent during that
period. Dale was a political activist, campaigning, for instance,
with the Unitarian Joseph Chamberlain, for compulsory, free
and non-sectarian education. In the passage below, however,
he is anxious lest in Dissent's new-found interest in
incarnational theology and social and political institutions it
should lose sight of that intense concern for the individual soul
which characterised an earlier period.

The tendency to Individualism, which is one of the
marks of the Evangelical movement, appears in other
directions. Although its leaders insisted very earnestly
on the obligation of individual Christian men to live a
devout and godly life, they had very little to say about
the relations of the individual Christian to the general
order of human society, or about the realization of the
kingdom of God in all the various regions of human
activity. As the Revival had no great ideal of the Church
as a Divine institution, it had no great ideal of the State
as a Divine institution; nor had it any great ideal of the
Divine order of the world. It had no such dreams as
came to an ancient Jewish saint of the glory of Christ as
the true Lord of the human race, and of the whole life of
the race, the King who will listen to the cry of the
oppressed and break in pieces the oppressor. It had no
eagerness to take possession of the realms of Art,
Science, Literature, Politics, Commerce, Industry, in
the name of their true Sovereign and Prince. Hence its
ethical ideal of the individual Christian was wanting in

wealth and variety; for the ethical perfection of the individual is determined by his relations to the Church and to the whole order of the world. . . .

With us Congregationalists, as I have said, the old Evangelical passion for saving men came to have associated with it, forty or fifty years ago, a passion for truth for its own sake, and the passion for truth found its principal exercise in the province of exegesis. That seems excellent; in itself it is very excellent.

But if we ministers, and our people care more for truth than our fathers cared, do we care for men less? Let us test ourselves. Are we as *anxious* – ministers and people – about men as our fathers were? On any theory of eschatology there is a dark and menacing future for those who have been brought face to face with Christ in this life and have refused to receive His salvation and to submit to His authority. I do not ask whether the element of fear has a great place in our *preaching*, but whether it has a great place in our *hearts* – whether we ourselves are afraid – whether the Christian people who have been trained by us are afraid – of what will come to men who do not believe in Christ; whether we, whether our people, are filled with an agonizing earnestness for their salvation.

And, secondly, do we and our people, as the result of the passion for truth, know the real meaning of the Bible better than our fathers knew it a hundred years ago? We may not make the same blunders in dealing with its form; but the form is unimportant compared with the substance; and the substance is to be mastered not merely by the help of Bible Dictionaries and Hand-books, but by deep and devout meditation.

R.W. Dale, *The Old Evangelicalism and the New*
(1889), pp.18–19; 26–28.

In passing, Dale alludes to the row over Biblical criticism which beset Congregationalist ministerial training in the 1840s. The die-hard stance of those in authority had led to the expulsion of several students. Dale himself had done much to bring the teaching of the Broad Church *Essays and Reviews* to Dissenting congregations but here he warns against the aridity of mere intellectualism.

One student who had been summarily dismissed from a Congregational seminary in 1851 for unorthodox views concerning the Biblical canon had his revenge in a novel written within two years of Dale's sermon. In *The Revolution in Tanner's Lane*, William Hale White ('Mark Rutherford') placed Congregationalism's decline in the 1840s. His representative mid-century Independent, aptly named Broad, is ruled by social considerations, intellectually feeble and morally lax. Determined to present Congregationalism as morally and spiritually moribund, White conveniently omits any mention of the forces already brewing within this branch of Dissent, as evidenced by Miall's paper, *The Nonconformist*. Both the tendency to arrange history to support his own views and the passage on hypocrisy in this excerpt mark the author as Eliot's disciple.

> The Reverend John Broad was certainly not of the Revival type. He was a big, gross-feeding, heavy person with heavy ox-face and large mouth, who might have been bad enough for anything if nature had ordained that he should have been born in a hovel at Sheepgate or in the Black Country. As it happened, his father was a woollen draper, and John was brought up to the trade as a youth; got tired of it, thought he might do something more respectable; went to a Dissenting College; took charge of a little chapel in Buckinghamshire; married early; was removed to Tanner's Lane, and became a preacher of the Gospel. He was moderate in all of what he called his "views;" neither ultra-Calvinist nor Arminian; not rigid upon Baptism, and certainly much unlike his lean and fervid predecessor, the Reverend James Harden, M.A., who was educated at Cambridge; threw up all his chances there when he became convinced of sin; cast in his lot with the Independents, and wrestled even unto blood with the world, the flesh, and the devil in Cowfold for thirty years, till he was gathered to his rest. A fiery, ardent, untamable soul was

Harden's, bold and uncompromising. He never
scrupled to tell anybody what he thought, and would
send an arrow sharp and swift through any iniquity, no
matter where it might couch. He absolutely ruled
Cowfold, hated by many, beloved by many, feared by
all – a genuine soldier of the Cross. Mr. Broad very
much preferred the indirect mode of doing good, and if
he thought a brother had done wrong, contented
himself with praying in private for him. He was,
however, not a hypocrite, that is to say, not an ordinary
novel or stage hypocrite. There is no such thing as a
human being simply hypocritical or simply sincere. We
are all hypocrites, more or less, in every word and every
action, and, what is more, in every thought. It is a
question simply of degree. Furthermore, there are
degrees of natural capacity for sincerity, and Mr. Broad
was probably as sincere as his build of soul and body
allowed him to be. Certainly no doubt as to the truth of
what he preached ever crossed his mind. He could not
doubt, for there was no doubt in the air; and yet he
could not believe as Harden believed, for neither was
Harden's belief now in the air.

Mark Rutherford, *The Revolution in Tanner's
Lane* (1887), Ch. 17.

Dissenting Worship

Preaching the Word was at the heart of Puritan Dissenting
tradition: a fact which seemed to confirm for High Anglicans
the importance of the Church's authority, as they observed the
fissiparousness of Dissenting sects. The career of the Particular
Baptist, Charles Haddon Spurgeon (1834–92), is illustrative of
the way in which one man's voice might suffice to create a
'local church' powerful enough to survive doctrinal splits.
Having started to preach at seventeen, by the time he was
nineteen Spurgeon's fame had reached London where his
permanent ministry was to be established. Personally
unprepossessing, short, squat and with pig-like eyes,

Spurgeon's lively, intelligent and emotionally varied manner of delivering the evangelical message won him congregations so large (sometimes well over 10 000) as to necessitate first an open-air ministry, then the hiring of secular auditoria and in 1861 the building of the Metropolitan Tabernacle. The publication of his weekly sermons formed a 'penny pulpit' reaching an even wider congregation. A Calvinist, who nevertheless believed in the unbaptised sharing in communion, Spurgeon dissociated his following from the Baptist Union in 1887 because of its tolerance of weakened doctrine.

Mr Spurgeon is not only popular; he represents the popularity of his time. He is as unlike the popular preacher of the past, as his Tabernacle, with its stage, pit, and galleries, is unlike Westminster Abbey. He is "The Times" of modern evangelism. Many of his sermons would make good leading articles, and in the power, the profusion, and the rapidity with which they were poured forth, we are reminded of the steam press and the electric telegraph. And not the less is he emblematic of the times, that in his case the pulpit is stripped of all its common accessories. It is doubtful if the squat and somewhat round figure of the preacher would admit of improvement by gown and cassock. In an age, impatient of all kinds of pretence, he is anything but a clerical fop. There is no cant or whining about him; he is natural as the day; and were it not for time and place, few would suppose from look, tone, or style, that they listened to a sermon. It is difficult, indeed, at first, to account for Mr Spurgeon's popularity. . . . It would be vain to fix on any one feature of the preacher in answer to this question. A combination of gifts as rare as startling, must account for his success in a career which, in the absence of any one of these gifts, might have proved a failure. There is the logical faculty appearing in the *lucidus ordo* of his discourses, combined with a fancy which brings up images at will, and scatters around the plainest subject a copiousness of illustration with the dexterity of the juggler, who brings, out of an old hat, an endless shower of flowers, feathers, and all sorts of unexpected things. Then there is the marvellous memory of the man, which, like some nimble servitor, seems to be always ready to supply him with the stories of his reading as they are needed; the sonorous voice, ringing like a church bell; the terse Saxon English of his style, the volubility of his elocution, joined with that perfect self-control, which prevents it from degenerating into declamation, and imparts to it something like the measured tramp of military precision. The whole structure of his sermons is conversational, but then it is conversation through a speaking-trumpet. The speaker is on fire throughout, but it is not in occasional flashes of flame that the fire appears, but in the sustained white-heat of the furnace. These are features well known to all who have listened to Spurgeon. One trait, however, though equally obvious, has not perhaps been so much marked as it deserves. We refer to what may be termed the *world-like* tone of his addresses. The world and the pulpit have long been at war with each other, and, it must be owned, with very varying success. If the preacher has at all his own way on Sunday, and launches his bolts at "the world" without any daring to gainsay him, the world in its turn takes its revenge on the pulpit during the week. Besides, no individual deems himself specially aimed at under that very general designation. Spurgeon, however, has the knack of making his shot tell upon the world. He has got into the way of talking for the gospel exactly as the world talks against it. . . . The worldling feels as if the tables had been turned upon him; the sceptic finds his cavils met with a loud guffaw, converting his sneer into the lugubrious look of injured innocence; and the profligate, shamed out of his habitual bravado, is half inclined to complain of being personally insulted. The pungency of this treatment is considerably enhanced by the tact with which the preacher singles out his victim, and holds him up before his audience for general inspection. In the best sense of the word, Mr Spurgeon deals largely in personalities; and as the fop in the play asks in high fume, "Do you

mean to call me an individual, Sir?" each man feels as if
he had been personally indicated. Sometimes this is
done by a familiar tap on the shoulder: "Away with all
that affectation of modesty which some good people
think to be so pretty, saying, 'I hope,' 'I trust,' 'But I
feel such doubts and gloomy misgivings.' *My dear Sir,
that is not humility!*" Sometimes it is by interpreting
the hidden language of the heart, thus: "How
dishonourable is it in you to say you believe in the
heart, and yet not make confession. *You are like a rat
behind the wainscot,* coming out just now and then,
when nobody is looking, and then running behind
again! *'What a degrading metaphor!'* you say. I meant
to degrade you by it, so as to drive you out of your
cowardice."

'The Rev. C.H. Spurgeon', *The British and Foreign
Evangelical Review*, Vol. 15 (1866), pp.195-96.

By the mid-nineteenth century hymn-singing found a place
in many forms of Christian worship but a strong eighteenth-
century tradition, seen in the contributions of Isaac Watts or
the brothers Wesley, and a partiality for this attractive feature
of worship, which might in other ways prove to be
aesthetically unrewarding, ensured the practice a special place
in Dissenting worship. The hymn reprinted below was
popularised by the American revivalists Moody and Sankey
during their 1874–75 mission. Only one of the famous *Sacred
Songs and Solos* was written by Sankey himself. Sankey's talent
lay in setting hymns to music and singing them to rapt
audiences.

"Rejoice with me, for I have found my sheep which was
lost." – LUKE XV.6.

There were ninety and nine that safely lay
    In the shelter of the fold;
But one was out on the hills away,
    Far off from the gates of gold,
Away on the mountains wild and bare,
Away from the tender Shepherd's care.

"Lord, Thou hast here Thy ninety and nine,
    Are they not enough for Thee?"
But the Shepherd made answer! "This of Mine
    Has wandered away from Me;
And although the road be rough and steep,
I go to the desert to find My sheep."

But none of the ransomed ever knew
    How deep were the waters crossed;
Nor how dark was the night that the Lord passed
        through
    Ere He found His sheep that was lost
Out in the desert He heard its cry,
Sick, and helpless, and ready to die.

"Lord, whence are those blood-drops all the way,
    That mark out the mountain's track?"
"They were shed for one who had gone astray
    Ere the Shepherd could bring him back."
"Lord, whence are Thy hands so rent and torn?"
"They are pierced to-night by many a thorn."

But all through the mountains, thunder-riven,
    And up from the rocky steep,
There arose a cry to the gate of heaven,
    "Rejoice! I have found My sheep!"
And the angels echoed around the throne,
"Rejoice, for the Lord brings back His own!"

E. Clephane, 'The Ninety and Nine', *Sacred Songs
and Solos*, compiled and sung by Ira D. Sankey
(1883).

The appeal of this hymn relies partly on its closeness to
ballad. It has a strong narrative line, sentimentally embellished,
and offers the opportunity for variety of tone in its exchanges
of dialogue. For the Revivalist it had the virtue of combining
conversion appeal, the promise of atonement and the chance
for corporate rejoicing.

The care expended by hymn-writers in shaping their verses
as a vehicle for correct doctrine was largely an irrelevance to
D.H. Lawrence, who recalls them for the feelings they evoked.

I think it was good to be brought up a Protestant: and among Protestants, a Nonconformist, and among Nonconformists, a Congregationalist. Which sounds pharisaic. But I should have missed bitterly a direct knowledge of the Bible, and a direct relation to Galilee and Canaan, Moab and Kedron, those places that never existed on earth. And in the Church of England one would hardly have escaped those snobbish hierarchies of class, which spoil so much for a child. And the Primitive Methodists, when I was a boy, were always having "revivals" and being "saved", and I always had a horror of being saved.

So, altogether, I am grateful to my "Congregational" upbringing. The Congregationalists are the oldest Nonconformists, descendants of the Oliver Cromwell Independents. They still had the Puritan tradition of no ritual. But they avoided the personal emotionalism which one found among the Methodists when I was a boy.

I liked our chapel, which was tall and full of light, and yet still; and colour-washed pale green and blue, with a bit of lotus pattern. And over the organ-loft, "O worship the Lord in the beauty of holiness," in big letters.

That was a favourite hymn, too:

O worship the Lord, in the beauty of holiness,
  Bow down before Him, His glory proclaim;
With gold of obedience and incense of lowliness
  Kneel and adore Him, the Lord is His name.

I don't know what the "beauty of holiness" is, exactly. It easily becomes cant, or nonsense. But if you don't think about it – and why should you? – it has a magic. The same with the whole verse. It is rather bad, really, "gold of obedience" and "incense of lowliness". But in me, to the music, it still produces a sense of splendour.

I am always glad we had the Bristol hymn-book, not Moody and Sankey. And I am glad our Scotch minister

on the whole avoided sentimental messes such as *Lead,
Kindly Light*, or even *Abide With Me*. He had a healthy
preference for healthy hymns.

> At even, ere the sun was set,
> The sick, O Lord, around Thee lay.
> Oh, in what divers pains they met!
> Oh, in what joy they went away!

And often we had "Fight the good fight with all thy
might".
In Sunday School I am eternally grateful to old Mr.
Remington, with his round white beard and his
ferocity. He made us sing! And he loved the martial
hymns:

> Sound the battle-cry,
> See, the foe is nigh.
> Raise the standard high
> For the Lord. . . .

Thirty-six years ago men, even Sunday School
teachers, still believed in the fight for life and the fun of
it. "Hold the fort, for I am coming." It was far, far from
any militarism or gunfighting. But it was the battle-cry
of a stout soul, and a fine thing too.

> Stand up, stand up for Jesus,
> Ye soldiers of the Lord.

Here is the clue to the ordinary Englishman – in the
Nonconformist hymns.

D.H. Lawrence, 'Hymns in a Man's Life', in
Selected Literary Critisism, ed. A. Beal (1961),
pp.9-11.

Lawrence's account of a Dissenting upbringing betrays the
way in which sectarian prejudices and pride can outlive any
doctrinal loyalty. The fine-sounding concluding phrase is

more than a little misleading when it is considered that many of the hymns he mentions were not of Dissenting origin. If Anglicans had been slow to recognise the appeal of hymn-singing, Dissent was swift to appropriate successful Anglican composition. Lawrence's Dissenting background continued to be of importance to him because these magical phrases, together with the symbols and rhythms of the Bible, provided him with a phraseology and register in which to convey 'the religious element inherent in all life . . . the sense of wonder'.

Separation from the World or Philistinism

The importance of the individual response to matters of conscience enshrined in Dissent could lead the believer in ever narrower paths and to ever smaller sects. Edmund Gosse's parents practised individualism with unremitting intensity. Gosse senior was a scientist of some distinction who had sought to reconcile the evidence of the rocks with the account of creation in Genesis in a notably eccentric manner (*Omphalos*, 1857). Eventually alienated by the hothouse life of spiritual agonising and gloom which dominated his childhood the son looks back on his parents' religious position as a negatively evolved elitism.

> It was a curious coincidence that life had brought both my parents along similar paths to an almost identical position in respect to religious belief. She had started from the Anglican standpoint, he from the Wesleyan, and each, almost without counsel from others, and after varied theological experiments, had come to take up precisely the same attitude towards all divisions of the Protestant Church, that, namely, of detached and unbiased contemplation. So far as the sects agreed with my Father and my Mother, the sects were walking in the light; wherever they differed from them, they had slipped more or less definitely into a penumbra of their own making, a darkness into which neither of my parents would follow them. Hence, by a process of selection, my Father and my Mother alike

had gradually, without violence, found themselves shut outside all Protestant communions, and at last they met only with a few extreme Calvinists like themselves, on terms of what may almost be called negation – with no priest, no ritual, no festivals, no ornament of any kind, nothing but the Lord's Supper and the exposition of Holy Scripture drawing these austere spirits into any sort of cohesion. They called themselves 'the Brethren', simply; a title enlarged by the world outside into 'Plymouth Brethren'.

E. Gosse, *Father and Son* (1907), pp.4-5.

Recognising the tension between his father's strict Calvinist dogma and his searing love for his only child, the son explains how his father managed to evolve the necessary qualifications to his theology of conversion.

In dealing with the peasants around him, among whom he was engaged in an active propaganda, my Father always insisted on the necessity of conversion. There must be a new birth and being, a fresh creation in God. This crisis he was accustomed to regard as manifesting itself in a sudden and definite upheaval. There might have been prolonged practical piety, deep and true contrition for sin, but these, although the natural and suitable prologue to conversion, were not conversion itself. . . .

But on some day, at some hour and minute, if life was spared to them, the way of salvation would be revealed to these persons in such an aspect that they would be enabled instantaneously to accept it. They would take it consciously, as one takes a gift from the hand that offers it. This act of taking was the process of conversion, and the person who so accepted was a child of God now, although a single minute ago he had been a child of wrath. The very root of human nature had to be changed, and, in the majority of cases, this change was sudden, patent, palpable.

I have just said 'in the majority of cases', because my

Father admitted the possibility of exceptions. The formula was, 'If any man hath not the Spirit of Christ, he is none of his.' As a rule, no one could possess the Spirit of Christ, without a conscious and full abandonment of the soul, and, this, however carefully led up to, and prepared for the tears and renunciations, was not, could not, be made, except at a set moment of time. . . .

But there was, or there might be, another class of persons, whom early training, separation from the world, and the care of godly parents had so early familiarized with the acceptable calling of Christ that their conversion had occurred, unperceived and therefore unrecorded, at an extraordinarily early age. It would be in vain to look for a repetition of the phenomenon in those cases. The heavenly fire must not be expected to descend a second time; the lips are touched with the burning coal once, and once only. If, accordingly, these precociously selected spirits are to be excluded because no new birth is observed in them at a mature age, they must continue outside in the cold, since the phenomenon cannot be repeated. When, therefore, there is not possible any further doubt of their being in possession of salvation, longer delay is useless, and worse than useless. The fact of conversion, though not recorded nor even recollected, must be accepted on the evidence of confession of faith, and as soon as the intelligence is evidently developed, the person not merely may, but should be accepted into communion, although still immature in body, although in years still even a child. This my Father believed to be my case, and in this rare class did he fondly persuade himself to station me.

Ibid, pp.199-203.

Somewhere between biography, autobiography and fiction, *Father and Son* demonstrates the difficulty of achieving emotional rather than intellectual detachment from such an upbringing. The serious critique the author comes near offering is sometimes undermined by the contrived comic effects he so carefully stages.

The cultural narrowness of much Dissenting life offended against the goal of 'harmonious perfection' that Matthew Arnold had substituted for his father's vision of a Broad State Church (see pp.56–57). For Matthew Arnold *The Nonconformist* became the symbol for the divisive parochialism of Dissent. His picture embodies the prejudice it had been Eliot's desire to challenge and wholly dismisses the alternative but equally valid culture to which Lawrence paid tribute.

> Notwithstanding the mighty results of the Pilgrim Fathers' voyage, they and their standard of perfection are rightly judged when we figure to ourselves Shakespeare or Virgil, – souls in whom sweetness and light, and all that in human nature is most humane, were eminent, – accompanying them on their voyage, and think what intolerable company Shakespeare and Virgil would have found them! In the same way let us judge the religious organisations which we see all around us. Do not let us deny the good and the happiness which they have accomplished; but do not let us fail to see clearly that their idea of human perfection is narrow and inadequate, and that the Dissidence of Dissent and the Protestantism of the Protestant religion will never bring humanity to its true goal. As I said with regard to wealth: Let us look at the life of those who live in and for it, – so I say with regard to the religious organisations. Look at the life imaged in such a newspaper as the *Nonconformist*, – a life of jealousy of the Establishment, disputes, tea-meetings, openings of chapels, sermons; and then think of it as an ideal of a human life completing itself on all sides, and aspiring with all its organs after sweetness, light, and perfection!

M. Arnold, *Culture and Anarchy* (1869), Ch. 1.

5 Doubt

This chapter aims to suggest some of the problematic questions behind the religious doubt which became part of the intellectual atmosphere of the last forty years of the century. As the dates of some of the extracts would indicate, disbelief and doubt did not make a sudden appearance in the 1860s but grew to be regarded as less in the nature of a personal sin or crime warranting excommunication from good society. Since it often appeared that it was only a question of degree that distinguished the beliefs of Broad Churchmen from 'honest doubters', this is perhaps understandable. Indeed sometimes it seemed as if sceptics stood more upon the moral self-righteousness of their position than did believers, but then it was moral doubt just as often as theological speculation which proved a decisive factor in the retreat from orthodoxy and this determined the calibre of much Victorian agnosticism. Not only did it seem dishonest to accept Christianity in the spirit of Pascal's wager but it became almost a moral imperative to offer resistance to a God who was sometimes represented as threatening eternal punishment as the ultimate deterrent to disbelief. The growing humanitarianism of Victorian ethics made such an idea intrinsically distasteful whilst encouraging the retention of that portion of Christianity which concentrated upon the life of Christ or the teachings of the Sermon on the Mount.

For many agnostics therefore the primary task became the need to prove that morality was not necessarily dependent upon religious belief. Until the two could be envisaged as divisible they were not anxious to proselytise, a reticence reinforced by the emotional nostalgia some felt for the comfort that belief had offered.

Doubt, like faith, it is important to recognise, is best seen as a process. In both cases post-conversion testimony tended to highlight critical moments or events but frequently it is impossible to detect which factor finally tipped the balance.

Biblical criticism and science were most frequently cited as forming the intellectual challenge to Christianity. Stated thus baldly it may seem surprising that they should have proved so alarming since neither was of itself new. The eighteenth century had seen attacks on the credibility of miracles and Lyell's work was in a sense only the culmination of the 'heroic age' of geology which began in about 1790. The Biblical or Higher Criticism emanating from Germany was of a different order in that it did not directly address dogmatic propositions but suggested *inter alia* that, seen as historical texts, the individual books of the Bible were the product of various writers and different periods. Moreover comparison with similarly received classical texts would suggest that certain facets of the Gospel narrative showed undoubted similarity to more universal myths. As *Essays and Reviews* (see pp.65–66) and *Lux Mundi* (see pp.47–49) showed, this mode of historical criticism did not of itself demand the instant repudiation of Christianity as a lie but it did require that the concept of divine inspiration be reinterpreted. For some, once verbal inspiration had been undermined and the historical basis of Christianity apparently discounted, the consequent rethinking could only seem to involve mental acrobatics more appropriate to wilful self-deception than theology.

Meanwhile geological scholarship had shown fundamentalist readings of Genesis to be in conflict with scientific fact. Once it had been shown that the earth's history long predated man's, the next stage was to discuss how man had arrived and what this new cosmogony did to his assumed theomorphic status. Chambers's *Vestiges of the Natural History of Creation* (1844) produced a readable, but scientifically negligible, stab in the direction of an evolutionary theory which remained compatible with deistic belief. Man's evolution from existing species of animal life was merely one more link in the laws of causation which God had specified in His original design. Inevitably this dismayed those who held to a beneficent God prepared to intervene in His universe in favour of the creature he had uniquely created in His own image. Darwin's *Origin of Species* became the symbolic text for the conflict of science and religion partly because of the sheer weight of scientific evidence he had collected and partly because his evolutionary theory rested its case upon natural selection rather than the purposive love of God.

For doubters and believers alike the complete amorality of this process often seemed too bleak to face and the meliorism adopted by some agnostics brought them closer than they might have wished to admit to those Christians who now spoke less of God's intervention in the Atonement and more of the Incarnation and His continuous presence in His creation.

Given the sense of loss which so often accompanied doubt, the subject more often received melancholy than humorous treatment in literature. Even the fiercely anti-Christian Swinburne or the flippantly anti-orthodox Samuel Butler did not satirise the state of disbelief or doubt. The finest apparent exception to this rule is a passage from Disraeli's *Tancred* in which the serious-minded hero first encounters 'The Revelations of Chaos'. A vacuous young society girl explains the contents of this parody of Chambers's *Vestiges* thus:

> 'You know, all is development. The principle is perpetually going on. First, there was nothing, then there was something; then I forget the next, I think there were shells, then fishes; then we came at last. And the next change there will be something very superior to us, something with wings. Ah! that's it: we were fishes, and I believe we shall be crows'.

> B. Disraeli, *Tancred* (1847), Book II, Ch. 9.

Disraeli could afford to mock because he simply could not take scientific materialism as a serious challenge to the semi-mystical religious synthesis for which the rest of the novel argues. The satirical vein of Mallock's *New Republic* (see pp.66–68), in which Ruskin, Pater, Arnold and Huxley appear, is again premised upon the absolute fatuity of their respective sceptical positions.

What remains striking when one sets these examples beside those of fellow authors adrift on the sea of doubt, such as Eliot, Rutherford or Hardy, is the absence of the secular indifference to which the twentieth century has accustomed us. For many of the writers the issue was never finally closed. As Browning's Bishop Blougram has it, unbelief, like belief, 'shakes us by fits'.

> Just when we are safest, there's a sunset touch,
> A fancy from a flower-bell, some one's death,
> A chorus ending from Euripedes, –
> And that's enough for fifty hopes and fears
> As old and new at once as nature's self,
> To rap and knock and enter in our soul,
> Take hands and dance there, a fantastic ring,
> Round the ancient idol, on his base again, –
> The grand Perhaps!
>
> R. Browning, 'Bishop Blougram's Apology' (1855),
> ll.182–90.

This ambivalence of approach was often more noticeable when secular visions of moral duty or progress were couched in the language of the old orthodoxy and the imagery and rhythms of the Bible were still relied upon for nuances and allusions which writers and readers, Christian and agnostic, could share.

The Role of Myth in the Gospels

The German philosopher–theologian, David Friedrich Strauss, published *Das Leben Jesu* in 1835–36. Its first full translation into English, undertaken by Mary Ann Evans (George Eliot) did not appear until 1846. In his preface Strauss explained the novelty of his critical approach. Eighteenth-century rationalists had concentrated on disproving the miraculous element of the Gospels and either produced even more fantastic naturalistic explanations or proceeded to claim that Christian faith was based on a lie. Strauss accepted it as axiomatic that miracles did not occur but devoted his attention to enquiring how it was that they came to be believed. Drawing on recent German historical and classical scholarship into comparative mythology, he argued for the role of myth as a poetic expression of spiritual truth. Since Strauss's work preceded effective scholarship investigating the extent of the Gospel's historic foundations, he tended to overplay the role of myth. George Eliot reported herself 'Strauss-sick – it made her ill dissecting the beautiful story of the crucifixion, and only the sight of her Christ-image, and picture made her endure it'. Despite his desire to produce a positive critique Strauss's own faith did not survive.

It appeared to the author of the work, the first half of which is herewith submitted to the public, that it was time to substitute a new mode of considering the life of Jesus, in the place of the antiquated systems of supranaturalism and naturalism. . . . The new point of view, which must take the place of the above, is the mythical. This theory is not brought to bear on the evangelical history for the first time in the present work: it has long been applied to particular parts of that history, and is here only extended to its entire tenor. It is not by any means meant that the whole history of Jesus is to be represented as mythical, but only that every part of it is to be subjected to a critical examination, to ascertain whether it have not some admixture of the mythical. The exegesis of the ancient church set out from the double presupposition: first, that the gospels contained a history, and secondly, that this history was a supernatural one. Rationalism rejected the latter of these presuppositions, but only to cling the more tenaciously to the former, maintaining that these books present unadulterated, though only natural, history. Science cannot rest satisfied with this half measure: the other presupposition must also be relinquished, and the inquiry must first be made whether in fact, and to what extent, the ground on which we stand in the gospels is historical. This is the natural course of things, and thus far the appearance of a work like the present is not only justifiable, but even necessary. . . . The author is aware that the essence of the Christian faith is perfectly independent of his criticism. The supernatural birth of Christ, his miracles, his resurrection and ascension, remain eternal truths, whatever doubts may be cast on their reality as historical facts. The certainty of this alone can give calmness and dignity to our criticism, and distinguish it from the naturalistic criticism of the last century, the design of which was, with the historical fact, to subvert also the religious truth, and which thus necessarily became frivolous. . . .

We distinguish by the name *evangelical mythus* a narrative relating directly or indirectly to Jesus, which may be considered not as the expression of a fact, but as the product of an idea of his earliest followers: such a narrative being mythical in proportion as it exhibits this character. The mythus in this sense of the term meets us, in the Gospel as elsewhere, sometimes in its pure form, constituting the substance of the narrative, and sometimes as an accidental adjunct to the actual history.

The pure mythus in the Gospel will be found to have two sources, which in most cases contributed simultaneously, though in different proportions, to form the mythus. The one source is, as already stated, the Messianic ideas and expectations existing according to their several forms in the Jewish mind before Jesus, and independently of him; the other is that particular impression which was left by the personal character, actions, and fate of Jesus, and which served to modify the Messianic idea in the minds of his people. The account of the Transfiguration, for example, is derived almost exclusively from the former source; the only amplification taken from the latter source being – that they who appeared with Jesus on the Mount spake of his decease. On the other hand, the narrative of the rending of the veil of the temple at the death of Jesus seems to have had its origin in the hostile position which Jesus, and his church after him, sustained in relation to the Jewish temple worship. Here already we have something historical, though consisting merely of certain general features of character, position etc.; we are thus at once brought upon the ground of the historical mythus.

The historical mythus has for its groundwork a definite individual fact which has been seized upon by religious enthusiasm, and twined around with mythical conceptions culled from the idea of the Christ. This fact is perhaps a saying of Jesus such as that concerning 'fishers of men' or the barren fig-tree, which now appear in the Gospels transmuted into marvellous histories: or, it is perhaps a real transaction or event taken from his life; for instance, the mythical traits in the account of the baptism were built upon such a reality. Certain of the miraculous histories may likewise have had some foundation in natural occurrences, which the narrative has either exhibited in a supernatural light, or enriched with miraculous incidents.

All the species of imagery here enumerated may justly be designated as mythi, . . . inasmuch as the unhistorical which they embody – whether formed gradually by tradition, or created by an individual author – is in each case the product of an *idea*. But for those parts of the history which are characterized by indefiniteness and want of connexion, by misconstruction and transformation, by strange combinations and confusion – the natural results of a long course of oral transmission; or which, on the contrary, are distinguished by highly coloured and pictorial representations, which also seem to point to a traditionary origin – for those parts the term *legendary* is certainly the more appropriate.

Lastly. It is requisite to distinguish equally from the mythus and the legend, that which, as it serves not to clothe an idea on the one hand, and admits not of being referred to tradition on the other, must be regarded as *the addition of the author*, as purely individual, and designed merely to give clearness, connexion, and climax, to the representation.

D.F. Strauss, *The Life of Jesus critically examined*, trans. G. Eliot (1846), Vol. I, pp.ix-xi; 85-87.

The Evidence of the Rocks

Charles Lyell, author of *Principles of Geology* (1830–33), remained a practising Anglican layman all his life. Yet his immense work, exploring the relentless uniformity of natural causation operating as far back as the evidence of geological strata could reveal carried with it theological, moral and emotional implications the author himself did not explore. The challenge to the time scale of creation given in Genesis or the diminution of Noah's flood caused no great difficulty to the majority of educated men, lay or clerical. However, even though Lyell concerned himself with the evolution of rock and plant life, not with animals or man, and even though he excluded the question of creation itself from his investigations, the general tenor of his writing disturbed sensitive readers like Tennyson and suggested that the popular prejudice which conceived science and religion as implacable foes was not altogether without foundation. Passing references speaking of the human race 'considered merely as consumers of a certain quantity of organic matter' (Vol. III, p.128) suggested a way of thought which took little account of the moral and spiritual features distinguishing man from the brute.

> Assuming the future duration of the planet to be indefinitely protracted, we can foresee no limit to the perpetuation of some of the memorials of man, which are continually entombed in the bowels of the earth or in the bed of the ocean, unless we carry forward our views to a period sufficient to allow the various causes of change, both igneous and aqueous, to remodel more than once the entire crust of the earth. *One* complete revolution will be inadequate to efface every monument of our existence; for many works of art might enter again and again into the formation of successive eras, and escape obliteration even though the very rocks in which they had been for ages imbedded were destroyed, just as pebbles included in the conglomerates of one epoch often contain the organized remains of beings which flourished during a prior era.
>   Yet it is no less true, as a late distinguished philosopher has declared, "that none of the works of a mortal being can be eternal." They are in the first place wrested from the hands of man, and lost as far as regards

their subserviency to his use, by the instrumentality of those very causes which place them in situations where they are enabled to endure for indefinite periods. And even when they have been included in rocky strata, when they have been made to enter as it were into the solid framework of the globe itself, they must nevertheless eventually perish; for every year some portion of the earth's crust is shattered by earthquakes or melted by volcanic fire, or ground to dust by the moving waters on the surface. . . .

As geologists, we learn that it is not only the present condition of the globe which has been suited to the accommodation of myriads of living creatures, but that many former states also have been adapted to the organization and habits of prior races of beings. The disposition of the seas, continents and islands, and the climates, have varied; the species likewise have been changed; and yet they have all been so modelled, on types analogous to those of existing plants and animals, as to indicate throughout a perfect harmony of design and unity of purpose. To assume that the evidence of the beginning or end of so vast a scheme lies within the reach of our philosophical inquiries, or even of our speculations, appears to be inconsistent with a just estimate of the relations which subsist between the finite powers of man and the attributes of an Infinite and Eternal Being.

C. Lyell, *Principles of Geology* (1835), 4th edn,
Vol. III, pp.279–80; Vol. IV, p.401.

Lyell's geological evidence indicated a time scale which had seen the disappearance of entire races of animal life and seemed directly to refute the Gospel account of a Providential God who cared for the fall of a sparrow and numbered the hairs of the head (Matthew 10.29–31). Material nature's grand indifference to spiritual being and purpose becomes a frightening mockery if viewed from the standpoint of man's delusive endeavours. Tennyson clings obstinately to the hope that a consolatory perspective does exist, though such comfort is diminished by its inaccessibility to mortal vision. It is worth turning back at this point to read the immediately preceding stanzas (see pp.72–73).

'So careful of the type?' but no.
    From scarpèd cliff and quarried stone
    She cries, 'A thousand types are gone:
I care for nothing, all shall go.

'Thou makest thine appeal to me:
    I bring to life, I bring to death:
    The spirit does but mean the breath:
I know no more.' And he, shall he,

Man, her last work, who seemed so fair,
    Such splendid purpose in his eyes,
    Who rolled the psalm to wintry skies,
Who built him fanes of fruitless prayer,

Who trusted God was love indeed
    And love Creation's final law –
    Though Nature, red in tooth and claw
With ravine, shrieked against his creed –

Who loved, who suffered countless ills,
    Who battled for the True, the Just,
    Be blown about the desert dust,
Or sealed within the iron hills?

No more? A monster then, a dream,
    A discord. Dragons of the prime,
    That tare each other in their slime,
Were mellow music matched with him.

O life as futile, then, as frail!
    O for thy voice to soothe and bless!
    What hope of answer, or redress?
Behind the veil, behind the veil.

Lord Tennyson, *In Memoriam* (1850), LVI. (This section was written 'some years before' 1844.)

Evolution by Natural Selection

By the time *On the Origin of Species by means of Natural Selection, or the Preservation of Favoured Races in the Struggle for Life* appeared in 1859 Darwin was no longer a Christian but a theist. The evolution of his own religious position which was to end in agnosticism had been gradual and affected by moral considerations, awareness of historical criticism and comparative religions as well as his scientific discoveries. Although *Origin of Species* was not overtly concerned with man and Darwin remained notoriously reluctant to discuss or declare his religious position, 'Darwinism' became a popular synonym for the scientific challenge to Christian orthodoxy. Darwin chose to conclude his book with a passage asserting that his theory was compatible with the argument from design, which deduced a beneficent Creator from examining His creation, but the evidence he provided of immutable laws controlling evolution certainly removed the Creator to the sidelines by denying the possibility of his subsequent benevolent interference. Moreover, as Darwin was prone at other times to feel, the pain and suffering involved in natural selection sat ill with a theist position.

Authors of the highest eminence seem to be fully satisfied with the view that each species has been independently created. To my mind it accords better with what we know of the laws impressed on matter by the Creator, that the production and extinction of the past and present inhabitants of the world should have been due to secondary causes, like those determining the birth and death of the individual. When I view all beings not as special creations, but as the lineal descendants of some few beings which lived long before the first bed of the Cambrian system was deposited, they seem to me to become ennobled. Judging from the past, we may safely infer that not one living species will transmit its unaltered likeness to a distant futurity. And of the species now living very few will transmit progeny of any kind to a far distant futurity; for the manner in which all organic beings are grouped, shows that the greater number of species in each genus, and all the species in many genera, have left no descendants, but have become utterly extinct. We can so far take a prophetic glance into futurity as to foretell that it will be the common and widely-spread species, belonging to the larger and dominant groups within each class, which will ultimately prevail and procreate new and dominant species. As all the living forms of life are the lineal descendants of those which lived long before the Cambrian epoch, we may feel certain that the ordinary succession by generation has never once been broken, and that no cataclysm has desolated the whole world. Hence we may look with some confidence to a secure future of great length. And as natural selection works solely by and for the good of each being, all corporeal and mental endowments will tend to progress towards perfection.

It is interesting to contemplate a tangled bank, clothed with many plants of many kinds, with birds singing on the bushes, with various insects flitting about, and with worms crawling through the damp earth, and to reflect that these elaborately constructed forms, so different from each other, and dependent upon each other in so complex a manner, have all been produced by laws acting around us. These laws, taken in the largest sense, being Growth and Reproduction; Inheritance which is almost implied by reproduction: Variability from the indirect and direct action of the conditions of life, and from use and disuse: a Ratio of Increase so high as to lead to a Struggle for Life, and as a consequence to Natural Selection, entailing Divergence of Character and the Extinction of less-improved forms. Thus, from the war of nature, from famine and death the most exalted object which we are capable of conceiving, namely, the production of the higher animals, directly follows. There is grandeur in this view of life with its several powers, having been originally breathed by the Creator into a few forms or into one; and that, whilst this planet has gone cycling on according to the fixed law of gravity, from so simple a beginning endless forms most beautiful and most wonderful have been, and are being evolved.

C. Darwin, *On the Origin of Species by means of Natural Selection* (1859), Ch. 53.

Huxley had embraced scepticism before he embarked upon his scientific career. Fired by enthusiasm for Darwin's evolutionary theory, he threw himself into the role of champion for scientific freedom. His rejoinder to Bishop Samuel Wilberforce's ridicule of Darwinism at the British Association meeting in Oxford in 1860 is perhaps the pithiest statement of his position. 'If . . . the question is put to me, would I rather have a miserable ape for a grandfather or a man highly endowed by nature and possessed of great means of influence and yet who employs these faculties and that influence for the mere purpose of introducing ridicule into a grave scientific discussion – I unhesitatingly affirm my preference for the ape'. In 1863 Huxley published lectures, initially delivered to working men, in which he succinctly presented the scientific evidence for man's being one in substance and structure with the ape.

Thoughtful men, once escaped from the blinding influences of traditional prejudice, will find in the lowly stock whence Man has sprung, the best evidence of the splendour of his capacities; and will discern in his long progress through the Past, a reasonable ground of faith in his attainment of a nobler Future.

They will remember that in comparing civilised man with the animal world, one is as the Alpine traveller, who sees the mountains soaring into the sky and can hardly discern where the deep shadowed crags and roseate peaks end, and where the clouds of heaven begin. Surely the awestruck voyager may be excused if, at first, he refuses to believe the geologist, who tells him that these glorious masses are, after all, the hardened mud of primeval seas, or the cooled slag of subterranean furnaces – of one substance with the dullest clay, but raised by inward forces to that place of proud and seemingly inaccessible glory.

But the geologist is right; and due reflection on his teachings, instead of diminishing our reverence and our wonder, adds all the force of intellectual sublimity to the mere æsthetic intuition of the uninstructed beholder.

T.H. Huxley, 'On the relations of man to the lower animals', *Evidence as to Man's Place in Nature* (1863), pp.154-55.

The lyrical celebration of a prospect of infinite biological and intellectual vistas opened up by evolution gave way in later life to a less optimistic view. In the following extract Huxley's denunciation of sentimental humanism has much in common with the secularised Protestantism of his early mentor, Carlyle.

I hear much of the "ethics of evolution." I apprehend that, in the broadest sense of the term "evolution," there neither is, nor can be, any such thing. The notion that the doctrine of evolution can furnish a foundation for morals seems to me to be an illusion, which has arisen from the unfortunate ambiguity of the term "fittest" in the formula, "survival of the fittest." We commonly use "fittest" in a good sense, with an understood connotation of "best;" and "best" we are apt to take in its ethical sense. But the "fittest" which survives in the struggle for existence may be, and often is, the ethically worst.

So far as I am able to interpret the evidence which bears upon the evolution of man as it now stands, there was a stage in that process when, if I may speak figuratively, the "Welt-geist" repented him that he had made mankind no better than the brutes, and resolved upon a largely new departure. Up to that time, the struggle for existence had dominated the way of life of the human, as of the other, higher brutes; since that time, men have been impelled, with gentle but steady pressure, to help one another, instead of treading one another mercilessly under foot; to restrain their lusts, instead of seeking, with all their strength and cunning, to gratify them; to sacrifice themselves for the sake of the ordered commonwealth, through which alone the ethical ideal of manhood can be attained, instead of exploiting social existence for their individual ends. Since that time, as the price of the high distinction of his changed destiny, man has lost the happy singleness of aim of the brute; and, from cradle to grave, that which he would not he does, because the cosmic process carries him away; and that which he would he does not, because the ethical stream of tendency is still but a rill.

It is the secret of the superiority of the best theological teachers to the majority of their opponents, that they substantially recognise these realities of things, however strange the forms in which they clothe their conceptions. The doctrines of predestination; of original sin; of the innate depravity of man and the evil fate of the greater part of the race; of the primacy of Satan in this world; of the essential vileness of matter; of a malevolent Demiurgus subordinate to a benevolent Almighty, who has only lately revealed himself, faulty as they are, appear to me to be vastly nearer the truth than the "liberal" popular illusions that babies are all born good and that the example of a corrupt society is responsible for their failure to remain so; that it is given to everybody to reach the ethical ideal if he will only try; that all partial evil is universal good; and other optimistic figments, such as that which represents "Providence" under the guise of a paternal philanthropist, and bids us believe that everything will come right (according to our notions) at last.

T.H. Huxley, 'An apologetic eirenicon',
Fortnightly Review, Vol. 52 (1892), pp.568-69.

The Ethical and Emotional Consequences of Doubt

The ease with which Huxley spoke of Christian ethical assumptions as a set of philosophical concepts separate from faith would have shocked doubters half a century earlier. James Anthony Froude bared his soul on the subject in that favourite

Victorian confessional form, the fictionalised spiritual autobiography. The identification of the *Nemesis of Faith*'s anti-hero, Sutherland, with his author led to Froude's resignation of his Oxford fellowship. Just as his older brother Hurrell, in whose shadow he had been brought up, had sought spiritual guidance and sanctuary in Keble, so James Anthony, in his search for spiritual authority, oscillated between Newman's Catholic anti-rationalism and Carlyle's unorthodox blend of Protestantism and German romanticism.

Newman grew up in Oxford, in lectures, and college chapels, and school divinity; Mr. Carlyle, in the Scotch Highlands, the poetry of Goethe. I shall not in this place attempt to acknowledge all I owe to this very great man; but, about three years before Newman's secession, chance threw in my way the "History of the French Revolution." I shall but caricature my feelings if I attempt to express them; and, therefore, I will only say that for the first time now it was brought home to me, that two men may be as sincere, as earnest, as faithful, as uncompromising, and yet hold opinions far asunder as the poles. I have before said that I think the moment of this conviction is the most perilous crisis of our lives; for myself, it threw me at once on my own responsibility, and obliged me to look for myself at what men said, instead of simply accepting all because they said it, I began to look about me to listen to what had to be said on many sides of the question, and try, as far as I could, to give it all fair hearing.

Newman talked much to us of the surrender of reason. Reason, first of everything, must be swept away, so daily more and more unreasonable appeared to modern eyes so many of the doctrines to which the Church was committed. As I began to look into what he said about it, the more difficult it seemed to me. What did it mean? Reason could only be surrendered by an act of reason. Even the Church's infallible judgements could only be received through the senses, and apprehended by reason; why, if reason was a false guide, should we trust one act of it more than another?

Fall back on human faculty somewhere we must, and how could a superstructure stone be raised on a chaff foundation? While I was perplexing myself about this, there came a sermon from him in St. Mary's, one much spoken of, containing a celebrated sentence. The sermon is that on the development of religious doctrine – the sentence is this: 'Scripture says the earth is stationary and the sun moves; science, that the sun is stationary and that the earth moves.' For a moment it seemed as if everyone present heard, in those words, the very thing they had all wished for and had long waited for – the final mesothesis for the reconciling of the two great rivals. Science and Revelation; and yet it was that sentence which at once cleared up my doubts the other way, and finally destroyed the faith I had in Newman, after 'Tract 90' had shaken it. For to what conclusion will it drive us? If Scripture does not use the word 'motion' in the sense in which common writers use it, it uses it in some transcendental sense by hypothesis beyond our knowledge. Therefore Scripture tells us nothing except what may be a metaphysical unattainable truth. But if Scripture uses one word in such sense without giving us warning, why not more words? . . .

The first part of this book in which Sutherland's moral objections to Christian dogma are outlined has a melodramatic sequel in which, having resigned his Anglican living, Sutherland travels to Italy where he embarks on a passionate affair with a married woman, whose child dies apparently as a consequence, thus proving that religion and morality are inseparable and that doubt has catastrophic consequences. The now Roman Catholic Newman reappears to save Sutherland from physical suicide but can offer no effective spiritual consolation. The desolation and futility of the novel's final paragraph go far to explain the energy with which later agnostics, like Leslie Stephen, preached their ethical gospel.

But Markham's new faith fabric had been reared upon the clouds of sudden violent feeling, and no air castle was ever of more unabiding growth; doubt soon sapped it, and remorse, not for what he had done, but for what he had not done; and amidst the wasted ruins of his life, where the bare bleak soil was strewed with wrecked purposes and shattered creeds; with no hope to stay him, with no fear to raise the most dreary phantom beyond the grave, he sunk down into the barren waste, and the dry sands rolled over him where he lay; and no living being was left behind him upon the earth, who would not mourn over the day which brought life to Markham Sutherland.

J.A. Froude, *Nemesis of Faith* (1849), pp.156–58;
226-27.

Leslie Stephen, an Anglican clergyman of Evangelical parentage, resigned his Cambridge fellowship in 1862. The precise reasons for his loss of faith are obscure, though it seems probable that the publication of *Origin of Species* and *Essays and Reviews* led him to feel that the logical development of the views they outlined was incompatible with dogmatic Christianity. The ethics of belief and disbelief, however, continued to preoccupy the agnostic Stephen. He was depressed by what he perceived as the intellectual and moral apathy of many of his contemporaries who continued to subscribe to Anglicanism whilst believing in little more doctrine than he did. Maurice's theology especially irritated him because it seemed to represent anti-rationalism triumphant. Working from an evolutionary model Stephen believed that Christianity would become acceptable to fewer and fewer and that it was therefore important to prove that Christianity and morality were not indivisible. In his attempt to preach an ethical gospel can be seen the moral commitment which typified high-minded Victorian agnosticism.

Let us suppose that Darwinism is triumphant at every point. Imagine it to be demonstrated that the long line of our genealogy can be traced back to the lowest organisms; suppose that our descent from the ape is conclusively proved, and the ape's descent from the tidal animal, and the tidal animal's descent from some ultimate monad, in which all the vital functions are reduced to the merest rudiments. . . . What is it that we have lost, and what have we acquired in its place? It is surely worth while to face the question boldly, and look into the worst fears that can be conjured up by these terrible discoverers. Probably, after such an inspection, the thought that will occur to any reasonable man will be, what does it matter? What possible difference can it make to me whether I am sprung from an ape or an angel? . . . There is still quite as much room as ever for the loftiest dreams that visit the imaginations of saints or poets. The mode in which we express ourselves must, of course, be slightly altered; but so long as the same instincts exist which sought gratification in the old language, we need not doubt but they will frame a new one out of the changed materials of thought. The fact that religion exists is sufficient demonstration that men feel the need of loving each other, of elevating the future and the past above the present, and of rising above the purely sensual wants of our nature; the need will exist just as much, whether we take one view or other of a set of facts which, on any hypothesis, happened many thousands of years before we were born, and in regard to which a contented ignorance is far from being an impossible frame of mind. . . .

There may, indeed, be no positive logical irreconcilability between orthodoxy and Darwinism. A little more straining of a few phrases which have proved themselves to be sufficiently elastic, and the first obvious difficulty may be removed. The first chapter of Genesis has survived Sir Charles Lyell; it may be stretched sufficiently to include Mr. Darwin. But in questions of this kind there is a kind of logical instinct which outruns the immediate application of the new theories. . . . Briefly it may be described as the substitution of a belief in gradual evolution for a belief in spasmodic action and occasional outbursts of creative energy; of the acceptance of the corollary that we must seek for the explanation of facts or ideas by tracing their history instead of accounting for them by some short *à priori* method; and thus of the adoption of the historical method in all manner of investigations into social, and political, and religious problems which were formerly solved by a much more summary, if not more satisfactory method. . . .

Give up supernatural interference, and man must be credited with the possession of virtuous instincts which gave the colouring to his theology. If our nature is essentially corrupt, it is consistent to believe that the scourge of hell-fire alone keeps us in order; but if man is not only the sufferer, but the inventor and wielder of the scourge, we must give up the dogma of corruption. If anyone chooses to say, I would sin but for my fear of hell, there is no arguing with him personally; but, accepting the scientific view, and therefore interrogating experience for what men have actually done, instead of interrogating our inner consciousness to find out what they should consistently do, we inevitably accept the conclusion that the virtuous instincts are the foundation, not the outgrowth, of the belief, and may therefore be expected to survive its destruction or transformation.

L. Stephen, 'Darwinism and Divinity' in *Essays on Freethinking and Plainspeaking* (1873), pp.75-77; 92-93; 106-107.

Not all doubters attained Stephen's intellectual or emotional certainty. Two examples are necessary to convey Arthur Hugh Clough's responses to his loss of faith. The elegiac tone and the satiric impulse which coexisted in his poetry were but one reflection of 'the dialogue of the mind with itself' which this most tortured of Victorian sceptics made it his business to explore. From Dr Arnold's education (see pp.56–61) Clough derived a conscience so refined that no intellectual position or moral commitment could be entertained without prompting speculation as to the involuntary impulses which might underlie them.

Whilst at Oxford Clough fell briefly under the influence of Tractarianism but in 1848 he felt his position as an Anglican fellow of a College untenable and resigned.

The extract below is an unfinished fragment. Hedged about with caution and articulated by negatives, an admission of minimal residual faith is wrung from the poet. His habit of considering and recasting Biblical narrative here renders the Lake of Galilee into a sea of doubt where Christ has become an impersonal force with verbal affinities to Matthew Arnold's 'the eternal not ourselves'.

> THAT there are powers above us I admit;
> It may be true too
> That while we walk the troublous tossing sea,
> That when we see the o'ertopping waves advance,
> And when [we] feel our feet beneath us sink,
> There are who walk beside us, and the cry
> That rises so spontaneous to the lips,
> The 'Help us or we perish,' is not nought,
> An evanescent spectrum of disease.
> It may be that in deed and not in fancy,
> A hand that is not ours upstays our steps,
> A voice that is not ours commands the waves,
> Commands the waves, and whispers in our ear,
> O thou of little faith, why didst thou doubt?
> At any rate –
> That there are beings above us, I believe,
> And when we lift up holy hands of prayer,
> I will not say they will not give us aid.

> A.H. Clough, Unfinished poem (1869).

From the fractured elliptical syntax and hesitancies of this poem we pass to the stingingly concise couplets of *The Latest Decalogue*. With deadly irony Clough captures the expediency of a wholly secular society which finds it convenient to use the traditional forms of the Old Testament decalogue and New Testament commandment to pronounce the currently acceptable code of conduct.

THOU shalt have one God only; who
Would be at the expense of two?
No graven images may be
Worshipped, except the currency:
Swear not at all; for for thy curse
Thine enemy is none the worse:
At church on Sunday to attend
Will serve to keep the world thy friend:
Honour thy parents; that is, all
From whom advancement may befall:

Thou shalt not kill; but needst not strive
Officiously to keep alive:
Do not adultery commit;
Advantage rarely comes of it:
Thou shalt not steal; an empty feat,
When it's so lucrative to cheat:
Bear not false witness; let the lie
Have time on its own wings to fly:
Thou shalt not covet; but tradition
Approves all forms of competition.

The sum of all is, thou shalt love,
If any body, God above:
At any rate shall never labour
More than thyself to love thy neighbour.

A.H. Clough, 'The Latest Decalogue' (1862).

'Dover Beach' is perhaps the age's finest poetic expression of the sense of desolation and disintegration brought about by the loss of faith's certainties. It is a more purely personal, emotional response than that of Froude's *Nemesis of Faith*, which, at base, seeks to give a paradigm of doubt's effects, or of Clough's *Easter Day* I, which though equally moving, also embodies a doctrinal argument.

The sea is calm to-night.
The tide is full, the moon lies fair

Upon the straits; on the French coast the light
Gleams and is gone; the cliffs of England stand,
Glimmering and vast, out in the tranquil bay.
Come to the window, sweet is the night-air!
Only, from the long line of spray
Where the sea meets the moon-blanched land,
Listen! you hear the grating roar
Of pebbles which the waves draw back, and fling,
At their return, up the high strand,
Begin, and cease, and then again begin,
With tremulous cadence slow, and bring
The eternal note of sadness in.

Sophocles long ago
Heard it on the Ægæan, and it brought
Into his mind the turbid ebb and flow
Of human misery; we
Find also in the sound a thought,
Hearing it by this distant northern sea.

The Sea of Faith
Was once, too, at the full, and round earth's shore
Lay like the folds of a bright girdle furled.
But now I only hear
Its melancholy, long, withdrawing roar,
Retreating, to the breath
Of the night-wind, down the vast edges drear
And naked shingles of the world.

Ah, love, let us be true
To one another! for the world, which seems
To lie before us like a land of dreams,
So various, so beautiful, so new,
Hath really neither joy, nor love, nor light,
Nor certitude, nor peace, nor help for pain;
And we are here as on a darkling plain
Swept with confused alarms of struggle and flight,
Where ignorant armies clash by night.

M. Arnold, 'Dover Beach' (written 1851).

Against the vastness and yet the insubstantiality of the landscape of nature and history is offered only the frail hope, not promise, of love's enduring truth. By the end of the poem those Wordsworthian 'gleams' have been extinguished without being replaced by philosophic consolations and the intimacy of the domestic scene has been effaced by the confusion and futility of the battlefield. Even the certainties and resolutions of poetic pattern are denied by the irregular rhymes and stanzaic forms of this 'tremulous cadence slow'.

Mary Augusta Ward, Dr Arnold's granddaughter and Matthew Arnold's niece, dramatised the spiritual pilgrimage from orthodox faith to doubt to a devout but secular faith, observable in many a late Victorian agnostic. Her hero takes up a country living after witnessing at Oxford both agnostic sainthood in the person of Mr Gray (a thinly-veiled portrait of the novel's dedicatee, T.H. Green) and moral and emotional paralysis as a consequence of disbelief in another tutor, Langham. The local squire presents a third version of faithlessness composed of German rationalism mated with French anti-clericalism. It is historical and comparative criticism that is mainly responsible for Elsmere's crisis of faith but Mrs Ward notes that evolution sharpens 'the comparative instinct – that tool, *par excellence* of modern science'. As the passage below makes clear the confession of doubt, no less than that of faith, is a religious experience for Elsmere.

> Robert stood still, and with his hands locked behind him, and his face turned like the face of a blind man towards a world of which it saw nothing, went through a desperate catechism of himself.
> 'Do I believe in God? Surely, surely! "Though He slay me yet will I trust in Him!" *Do I believe in Christ?* Yes, – in the teacher, the martyr, the symbol to us Westerns of all things heavenly and abiding, the image and pledge of the invisible life of the spirit – with all my soul and all my mind!
> '*But in the Man-God*, the Word from Eternity, – in a wonder-working Christ, in a risen and ascended Jesus, in the living Intercessor and Mediator for the lives of His doomed brethren?'

He waited, conscious that it was the crisis of his history, and there rose in him, as though articulated one by one by an audible voice, words of irrevocable meaning.

'Every human soul in which the voice of God makes itself felt, enjoys, equally with Jesus of Nazareth, the divine sonship, and *"miracles do not happen!"* '. ...

The lane darkened round him. Not a soul was in sight. The only sounds were the sounds of a gently breathing nature, sounds of birds and swaying branches and intermittent gusts of air rustling through the gorse and the drifts of last year's leaves in the wood beside him. He moved mechanically onward, and presently, after the first flutter of desolate terror had passed away, with a new inrushing sense which seemed to him a sense of liberty – of infinite expansion.

Suddenly the trees before him thinned, the ground sloped away, and there to the left on the westernmost edge of the hill lay the square-stone rectory, its windows open to the evening coolness, a white flutter of pigeons round the dovecote on the side lawn, the gold of the August wheat in the great cornfield showing against the heavy girdle of oak-wood.

Robert stood gazing at it, – the home consecrated by love, by effort, by faith. The high alternations of intellectual and spiritual debate, the strange emerging sense of deliverance, gave way to a most bitter human pang of misery.

'Oh God! My wife – my work!' ...

Mrs Humphry Ward, *Robert Elsmere* (1888),
Ch. 26.

The response of his Evangelical wife to his declaration of a belief devoid of the supernatural provides a sensitive record of the chasm of emotional anguish which sometimes opened between doubters whose moral calibre forced them to renounce a tacit lie and the truly pious orthodox to whom such a confession seemed a denial of all that gave life value. Darwin, who had discussed with his father the question of voicing his doubts to his prospective wife, later recorded, 'My father advised me to conceal carefully my doubts, for he said he had known extreme misery thus caused with married persons'.

'I cannot follow all you have been saying,' she said, almost harshly. 'I know so little of books, I cannot give them the place you do. You say you have convinced yourself the Gospels are like other books, full of mistakes, and credulous, like the people of the time; and therefore you can't take what they say as you used to take it. But what does it all quite mean? Oh, I am not clever – I cannot see my way clear from thing to thing as you do. If there are mistakes, does it matter so – so – terribly to you?' and she faltered. 'Do you think *nothing* is true because something may be false? Did not – did not – Jesus still live, and die, and rise again? – *can* you doubt – *do* you doubt – that He rose – that He is God – that He is in heaven – that we shall see Him?'

She threw an intensity into every word, which made the short, breathless questions thrill through him, through the nature saturated and steeped as hers was in Christian association, with a bitter accusing force. But he did not flinch from them.

'I can believe no longer in an incarnation and resurrection,' he said slowly, but with a resolute plainness. 'Christ is risen in our hearts, in the Christian life of charity. Miracle is a natural product of human feeling and imagination; and God was in Jesus – pre-eminently, as He is in all great souls, but not otherwise – not otherwise in kind than He is in me or you.'

His voice dropped to a whisper. She grew paler and paler.

'So to you' – she said presently in the same strange altered voice. 'My father – when I saw that light on his face before he died, when I heard him cry, "Master, *I come!*" was dying – deceived – deluded. Perhaps even,' and she trembled, 'you think it ends here – our life – our love?'

Ibid, Ch. 28.

To pass from the acute misery of Clough's lines 'We are most hopeless who had once most hope / We are most wretched that had most believed / Christ is not risen' or from Elsmere's agonisings to Ernest Pontifex's easy certainties in Samuel Butler's novel *The Way of All Flesh* is to experience a moral revolution. High-minded Victorian agnosticism has given way to the brasher notes of self-confident progressivism. Butler's own faith had dropped from him comparatively easily, though it left a residue of bitterness against the claustrophobic formalism of his Low Church upbringing. Subsequently he provided a host of reasons, scientific and historical, for his lapse but it seems to have been prompted by the sudden change involved in a voyage to New Zealand rather than by the logical pursuit of intellectual dissatisfaction. Ernest Pontifex's circumstances are changed even more abruptly when he is imprisoned for corrupting a young woman in the course of his Anglican ministry.

Perhaps the shock of so great a change in his surroundings had accelerated changes in his opinions, just as the cocoons of silkworms, when sent in baskets by rail, hatch before their time through the novelty of heat and jolting. But however this may be, his belief in the stories concerning the Death, Resurrection and Ascension of Jesus Christ, and hence his faith in all the other Christian miracles, had dropped off him once and for ever. The investigation he had made in consequence of Mr Shaw's rebuke, hurried though it was, had left a deep impression upon him, and now he was well enough to read he made the New Testament his chief study, going through it in the spirit which Mr Shaw had desired of him: that is to say as one who wished neither to believe nor disbelieve, but cared only about finding out whether he ought to believe or no. The more he read in this spirit the more the balance seemed to lie in favour of unbelief, till, in the end, all further doubt became impossible, and he saw plainly enough that, whatever else might be true, the story that Christ had died, come to life again, and been carried from earth through clouds into the heavens, could not now be accepted by

unbiased people. It was well he had found it out so
soon. In one way or another it was sure to meet him
sooner or later. He would probably have seen it years
ago if he had not been hoodwinked by people who were
paid for hoodwinking him. What should he have done,
he asked himself, if he had not made his present
discovery till years later, when he was more deeply
committed to the life of a clergyman? Should he have
had the courage to face it, or would he not more
probably have evolved some excellent reason for
continuing to think as he had thought hitherto? Should
he have had the courage to break away even from his
present curacy?

He thought not, and knew not whether to be more
thankful for having been shown his error or for having
been caught up and twisted round so that he could
hardly err farther, almost at the very moment of his
having discovered it. The price he had had to pay for
this boon was light as compared with the boon itself.
What is too heavy a price to pay for having duty made at
once clear and easy of fulfilment instead of very
difficult? He was sorry for his father and mother, and
he was sorry for Miss Maitland, but he was no longer
sorry for himself.

S. Butler, *The Way of All Flesh* (1903), Ch. 64.

As the opening image suggests, Butler is at pains to imply
that such changes merely throw evolutionary inevitability into
clear relief. Justified by a linear view of history, his hero finds
no trouble in dismissing those who still profess Christianity as
hypocrites and shows no comprehension of the quandary
which might result when moral scruple was finely bound up
with emotional attachment or intellectual perplexities.

Chronological Table

Date	Contemporary events	Publications
1825		S.T. Coleridge, *Aids to Reflection*
1827		J. Keble, *Christian Year*
1828	Repeal of Test and Corporation Acts	
1829	Roman Catholic Emancipation Act passed	
1830		C. Lyell, *Principles of Geology*
1832	Great Reform Act passed; Rev. Edward Irving dismissed from Scottish Church for heresy	
1833	Irish Church Bill raised disestablishment issue; Abolition of Slavery; Keble's Sermon on National Apostasy – beginning of the Oxford Movement	T. Arnold, *Principles of Church Reform* *Tracts for the Times* begun (completed 1841)
1836	Tractarians secure condemnation of Hampden's (Oxford's Regius Professor of Divinity) views; Charter granted to University College, London, enabling the taking of degrees without religious qualifications; Church Rates Abolition Society founded	
1838		R.H. Froude, *Remains*
1841	Anti-Corn Law Convention of Dissenting ministers	*The Nonconformist* first appeared; *Tract XC*
1842	Bishop Blomfield's Charge attempted to regulate liturgical practices	
1843	Disruption of the Church of Scotland	

Date	Contemporary events	Publications
1844	Anti-State Church Association formed (renamed Society for the Liberation of Religion from State Control in 1853)	R. Chambers, *Vestiges of the Natural History of Creation*
1845	Maynooth debates (over government grant to RC seminary in Ireland); Newman's secession to Rome	
1846	The National Secular Society founded	D.F. Strauss's *Das Leben Jesu* (1835) translated into English
1847	Hampden's bishopric contested; Shaftesbury's Ten Hours Bill passed (regulating child labour in factories)	C. Brontë, *Jane Eyre*
1848	Christian Socialist Movement founded; Anglican Community of the Sisters of Mercy (at Exeter) formed	C. Kingsley, *Yeast*
1849	Wesleyan Methodism split by Conference expulsion of radical critics	
1850	Gorham Judgement – mainly lay court legislated on an ecclesiastical matter and allowed a wide divergence of belief to be compatible with Anglicanism; 'Papal aggression' – establishment of Roman Catholic hierarchy in England; Ritualist riots at St Barnabas, Pimlico and St Paul's, Knightsbridge	Lord Tennyson, *In Memoriam*; C. Kingsley, *Alton Locke*
1851	Religious Census first taken	
1853	F.D. Maurice dismissed from King's College, London, for heretical views in *Theological Essays*	C.M. Yonge, *Heir of Redclyffe*
1857		A. Trollope, *Barchester Towers*; G. Eliot, *Scenes of Clerical Life*; T. Hughes, *Tom Brown's Schooldays*

Date	Contemporary events	Publications
1859		C. Darwin, *Origin of Species*; G. Eliot, *Adam Bede*
1860		*Essays and Reviews*
1861		*Hymns Ancient and Modern*
1862	Bicentenary of the Act of Uniformity	
1863		T.H. Huxley, *Man's Place in Nature*
1864		J.H. Newman, *Apologia pro Vita Sua*
1865	Privy Council decision in favour of Colenso	
1868	Abolition of Church Rate	
1869	Disestablishment of the Church of Ireland	M. Arnold, *Culture and Anarchy*
1870	Doctrine of Papal Infallibility proclaimed	
1871	University religious tests abolished	
1872	Nonconformist Conference on education	
1874	Public Worship Regulation Act – to curb Anglo-Catholic excesses (ineffective)	
1875	Moody and Sankey revivalism achieved national success	
1878	Salvation Army founded	
1886	Bradlaugh became first avowedly atheist MP to take his seat	
1887	'Down Grade' controversy – Spurgeon left Baptist Union because of its laxity over Calvinist doctrines	
1888		Mrs Humphry Ward, *Robert Elsmere*
1889		*Lux Mundi*
1903		S. Butler, *The Way of All Flesh*

Bibliography

Primary Sources

Arnold, Matthew, *Culture and Anarchy*, ed. R.H. Super (Ann Arbor, 1965)
——, *The Poems of Matthew Arnold*, ed. K. Allott (London, 1965)
Arnold, Thomas, *Christian Life, its course, its hindrances and its helps*, ed. Mrs W.E. Forster, 6 vols (London, 1878)
British Foreign and Evangelical Review, Vol. 15 (1866), pp.191-208
Brontë, Anne, *The Poems of Anne Bronte*, ed. E. Chitham (London, 1979)
Brontë, Charlotte, *Jane Eyre*, eds J. Jack and M. Smith (Oxford, 1969)
Browning, Robert, *Browning: The Poetical Works 1833-64*, ed. I. Jack (London, 1970)
Butler, Samuel, *The Way of All Flesh*, eds H.F. Jones and A. Bartholomew (London, 1925)
Clough, Arthur Hugh, *The Poems of Arthur Hugh Clough*, eds H.F. Lowry, A.L.P. Norrington and F.L. Mulhauser (Oxford, 1951)
Coleridge, Samuel Taylor, *Aids to Reflection and Confessions of an Inquiring Spirit*, Bohn's Library, (1884)
——, *On the Constitution of Church and State*, ed. K. Coburn (Princeton, 1976)
Conybeare, William John, 'Church Parties', *Edinburgh Review*, Vol. 98 (1853), pp.273-342
Dale, Robert William, *The Old Evangelicalism and the New* (London, 1889)
Darwin, Charles Robert, *On the Origin of Species by means of Natural Selection* (London, 1910)
Disraeli, Benjamin, *Tancred or The New Crusade*, Bradenham edn (London, 1927)
'Eliot, George' (Mary Ann Evans), *Adam Bede* and *Scenes of Clerical Life*, Cabinet edn, 24 vols (Edinburgh, 1878-85)
Froude, James Anthony, *The Nemesis of Faith* (London, 1849)
Gore, Charles (ed.), *Lux Mundi* (London, 1889)
Gosse, Edmund, *Father and Son* (London, 1907)
Havergal, Frances Ridley, *The Poetical Works of Frances Ridley Havergal* (London, 1884)

Hopkins, Gerard Manley, *The Poems of Gerard Manley Hopkins*, 4th edn, eds W.H. Gardner and N.H. Mackenzie (London, 1967)

Hughes, Thomas, *Tom Brown's Schooldays* (Cambridge, 1857)

Huxley, Thomas Henry, 'An Apologetic Eirenicon', *Fortnightly Review*, Vol. 52 (1892) pp.568–69

——, *Evidence as to Man's Place in Nature* (London, 1863)

Jowett, Benjamin, 'On the Interpretation of Scripture' in *Essays and Reviews*, 5th edn (1861), pp.330-433

Keble, John, *The Christian Year*, Everyman's Library (London, 1914)

Kingsley, Charles, *Yeast: A Problem* (London, 1902)

Lawrence, David Herbert, *David Herbert Lawrence: Selected Literary Criticism*, ed. A. Beal (London, 1961)

Liddon, Henry Parry, *Life of Edward Bouverie Pusey*, 4 vols (London, 1893–97)

Lyell, Charles, *Principles of Geology*, 4th edn, 4 vols (London, 1835)

Mallock, William Hurrell, *The New Republic* (Leicester, 1975)

Maurice, Frederick Denison, *The Kingdom of Christ*, 3rd edn, 2 vols (London, 1883)

Newman, John Henry, *Loss and Gain: The Story of a Convert* (London, 1896)

——, 'The State of Religious Parties', *The British Critic* (April 1839), pp.395–426

——, *Tract 73: The Rationalistic and the Catholic Spirit Compared* (1839)

The Nonconformist, 19 May 1841

Pattison, Mark, *Memoirs* (London, 1885)

Prothero, Rowland Edmund, *Letters and Verses of A.P. Stanley* (London, 1895)

Purchas, John, *The Directorium Anglicanum* (London, 1858)

Pusey, Edward Bouverie, *A Course of Sermons on Solemn Subjects delivered at St. Saviour's, Leeds* (Oxford, 1845)

Russell, George William Erskine, *The Household of Faith* (London, 1902)

'Rutherford, Mark' (William Hale White), *The Revolution in Tanner's Lane* (London, 1887)

Ryle, John Charles, *Evangelical Religion: what it is, and what it is not* (London, 1867. rpt 1954)

Sacred Songs and Solos, ed. I.D. Sankey (London, 1883)

Speeches of the Earl of Shaftesbury (London, 1856)

Stanley, Arthur Penrhyn, 'Judgement on *Essays and Reviews*', *Edinburgh Review*, Vol. 130 (1861)

Stephen, Leslie, *Essays on Freethinking and Plainspeaking* (London, 1873)

Strauss, David Friedrich, *The Life of Jesus critically examined*, trans. G. Eliot, 3 vols (London, 1846)
Tennyson, Alfred, Lord *The Poems of Tennyson*, ed. C. Ricks (London, 1969)
Tracts for the Times by Members of the University of Oxford, 6 vols (1834–41)
Trollope, Anthony, *Barchester Towers* (London, 1925)
——*Clergymen of the Church of England* (London, 1866)
Ward, Mrs Humphry (Mary Augusta), *Robert Elsmere*, 3 vols (London, 1888)
Wilberforce, William, *A Practical View of the Prevailing Religious System of Professed Christians, in the Higher and Middle Classes in this country, contrasted with real Christianity*, 2nd edn (London, 1797)
Yonge, Charlotte Mary, *The Daisy Chain* (London, 1856)

Secondary Sources

For more detailed discussion of the literature available see the *Pelican Guide to Modern Theology*, Vol. II (London, 1969), pp.307-342 and Elisabeth Jay (ed.), *The Evangelical and Oxford Movements* (Cambridge, 1983)

Baker, J.E., *The Novel and the Oxford Movement* (Princeton, 1932)
Balleine, G.R., *A History of the Evangelical Party in the Church of England* (1908); new edn (London, 1951)
Brett, R.L. (ed.), *Poems of Faith and Doubt* (London 1965)
Briggs, J.H.Y. and Sellers, I., *Victorian Nonconformity* (London, 1972)
Burrow, J.W., 'Faith, doubt and unbelief' in *The Victorians*, ed. L. Lerner (London, 1978), pp.153-73.
Chadwick, O. (ed.), *The Mind of the Oxford Movement* (London, 1960)
——, *The Victorian Church*, 2 vols (London, 1966)
Chapman, R., *Faith and Revolt: Studies in the literary influence of the Oxford Movement* (London, 1970)
Christensen, T., *Origin and history of Christian Socialism, 1848–54* (Aarhus, 1962)
Church, R.W., *The Oxford Movement: Twelve Years, 1833–1845* (London, 1891)
Cockshut, A.O.J., *Religious Controversies of the Nineteenth Century* (London, 1966)

Cockshut, A.O.J., *The Unbelievers: English Agnostic Thought 1840–1890* (London, 1964)

Cosslett, T., *Science and Religion in the Nineteenth Century* (Cambridge, 1984)

Cunningham, V., *Everywhere Spoken Against: Dissent in the Victorian Novel* (Oxford, 1975)

Davie, D., *A gathered church, the literature of the English dissenting interest, 1700–1930* (London, 1976)

Davies, H., *Worship and Theology in England*, Vols 3 and 4 (Princeton and London, 1961, 1962)

Davies, R. and Rupp, G. (eds) *A History of the Methodist Church II* (London, 1978)

De Laura, D.J., *Hebrew and Hellene in Victorian England: Newman, Arnold and Pater* (Austin, Texas, 1969)

Fairchild, H.N., *Religious Trends in English Poetry*, Vols II and IV (New York, 1942, 1957)

Fairweather, E. (ed.), *The Oxford Movement* (New York, 1964)

Flindall, R.P. (ed.), *The Church of England, 1815–1948: A Documentary History* (London, 1972)

Houghton, W., *The Victorian Frame of Mind 1830–1870* (New Haven, Conn., 1957)

Irvine, W., *Apes, Angels and the Victorians* (London, 1956)

Jay, E., *The Religion of the Heart: Anglican Evangelicalism and the Nineteenth-Century Novel* (Oxford, 1979)

Jones, R.T., *Congregationalism in England, 1662–1962* (London, 1962)

Maison, M., *Search Your Soul Eustace: A survey of the religious novel in the Victorian Age* (London, 1961)

Newsome, D., *The Parting of Friends* (London, 1966)

Prickett, S., *Romanticism and Religion: The Tradition of Coleridge and Wordsworth in the Victorian Church* (Cambridge, 1976)

Reardon, B.M.G., *From Coleridge to Gore, a century of religious thought in Britain* (London, 1971)

Rowell, D.G., *The Vision Glorious: Themes and Personalities of the Catholic Revival in Anglicanism* (Oxford, 1983)

Sellers, I., *Nineteenth-Century Nonconformity* (London, 1977)

Tennyson, G.B., *Victorian Devotional Poetry: the Tractarian Mode* (Cambridge, Mass., 1981)

Thompson, D.M. (ed.), *Nonconformity in the Nineteenth Century* (London, 1972)

Ward, W.R., *Religion and Society in England, 1790–1850* (London, 1972)

Willey, B., *Nineteenth-Century Studies* (London, 1949)

Willey, B., *More Nineteenth-Century Studies: a group of honest doubters* (London, 1956)

Wolff, R.L., *Gains and Losses: Novels of Faith and Doubt in Victorian England* (New York, 1977)

Index